To Jimmy

Happy Birthday

Amy.

The Dog Lovers' Pocket Book

Joan Palmer

Bloomsbury Books · London

First published by Eric Dobby Publishing Ltd.,
12 Warnford Road, Orpington, Kent BR6 6LW.

This edition published by Bloomsbury Books, an imprint of
The Godfrey Cave Group, 42 Bloomsbury Street, London, WC1B 3QJ, 1993

Printed and bound in Great Britain by
BPCC Hazell Books Ltd

Member of BPCC Ltd

ISBN 1 85471 302 7

CONTENTS

DEDICATION

The author would like to dedicate this work to her late husband, Doug Palmer-Moore and 'Bertie' the Chihuahua who stated it all; not forgetting 'Marius' (Bomlitz Petrouchka), the French Bulldog, and 'Narnia' (Nanimo Narnia of Pesaro) the Chinese Crested bitch, who are with her today, and whose pictures appear in the Almanac.

ACKNOWLEDGEMENTS

The author would like to thank Terry Whitham for allowing her to reproduce his photographs in this book.

Terry, who describes himself as 'an eligible bachelor from Sheffield', has been photographing dogs for more than 20 years. He is a regular contributor to numerous overseas publications and to the British *PetDogs* Magazine.

Terry does not own a dog, but enjoys making friends with those he meets on the dog show circuit.

INTRODUCTION

Dogs, for ease of classification, are usually categorised in groups, according to the task for which they were bred: e.g. terriers (which were bred to go to ground), hounds, gundogs and working dogs, such as sheepdogs. This in turn enables the buyer to make the right choice. A list at the back of the book gives every breed under the appropriate group.

The main part of this book lists the breeds alphabetically, for easy reference. In all cases, however, the character and origin of the breed are emphasised. Readers will thus be able to earmark those varieties which could best fulfil the role they have in mind, whether they intend to keep a dog as a pet-companion, a worker or a guard. The Almanac also gives each variety's exercise, feeding and space requirements.

There is a valuable section on the care of dogs, while the author reminds her readers to be prepared to travel. It should be possible to buy a Chihuahua in a city, but the breeder of a larger working variety is more likely to live well off the beaten track.

ANCESTORS OF THE DOG

The evolution of the dog traces back to the miacis, a small, tree-climbing carnivore, something like a weasel, which existed more than fifty million years ago.

It is however the tomarctus, a fox-like creature, which appeared some thirty-five million years later, that is recognised as the father of true canids (or canines). The Latin words *Canis Familiaris* are used to describe the Dog Family.

By the middle of the Pleistocene age about five million years ago, the tomarctus had disappeared, but wolves and jackals had become established.

Generally it is accepted that the domestic dog originated some 11,000 years ago in the Middle East, and that it had a common ancestor in the wolf and possibly the jackal. It is unlikely that fox blood was added.

The first identifiable remains of a pure bred dog were those of a Saluki, a breed which took its name from the town of Saluk in the Yemen.

THE DOMESTIC DOG

One can but guess how the bond between man and dog came about. Doubtless dog was attracted to the camp fire of early man by the promise of food and warmth. Man may have thrown it a scrap or two thereby gradually earning its friendship and trust. Later, the realisation would have dawned that this creature, once wholly tamed, might prove of worth as a companion, hunter and guard.

It was from wild dogs that man made the first crude attempts at selective breeding, drawing on the desired points and characteristics of dogs at hand until a uniform type had been established.

The recorded history of dogs for a thousand years, which begins with the work of Xenophon (c430 – c350BC), reveals that only hunting, or otherwise 'useful', dogs were produced. Although an encyclopaedia of dogs was published in Nuremberg in 1685, the first mention of pet, or toy dogs in Britain is accredited, in 1560, to the Cambridge scholar, John Caius.

The oldest pure breed in Britain is reckoned to be the Cardigan Welsh Corgi, which traces back to dogs brought to Wales by the Celts from the Black Sea area around 1200BC. But the Welsh Corgi was a cattle dog and therefore a 'useful' breed.

DOG
BREEDS

Affenpinscher

Characteristics: A comical, monkey-like little dog that is an excellent ratter and guard despite its small size. Affectionate and intelligent.

Origin: Prior to 1896 Affenpischers and Miniature Pinschers were regarded as one and the same. However, at the Berlin show in that year it was decided that, henceforth, the long coated variety should be known as the Affenpinscher. *Affen* is the German word for 'monkey'. In recent years the breed has been increasingly represented in British show classes.

Grooming: A daily brush is all that is necessary to keep this ragamuffin of a dog smart and healthy.

Exercising: Terrier-like, the Affenpinscher will walk its owners off their feet, if that is their wish, or be content with a walk around the park.

Colouring: Black. Grey shading is allowed.

Desired qualities: A rough, harsh coat, short straight back, and a head that is fairly small in proportion to the body.

Drawbacks: None known.

Afghan Hound

Characteristics: A glamorous breed that is loyal and affectionate, but needs space and knowledgeable handling.

Origin: Credited with being one of the animals taken into the Ark by Noah. Certainly it has existed for thousands of years in the Middle East, though present day thought is that it was crossed with the Saluki. At any rate a Greyhound type dog found its way from Persia to Afghanistan where it grew a long coat as protection against the colder climate.

Grooming: Not a breed to consider unless you are prepared for a good daily grooming session, preferably using a Mason Pearson type brush, with real bristle. You will also need to use a coat lubricant.

Exercising: Plenty. You may like to join an Afghan breed club that arranges Afghan Hound racing on a Sunday afternoon.

Colouring: All colours acceptable.

Desired qualities: Long, not too narrow skull, dark eyes, (golden eyes not objected to), level back of moderate length and long, sloping shoulders.

Drawbacks: This dog does not like to be teased. Needs firm, but gentle handling.

Airedale Terrier

Characteristics: The largest 'King' of the terriers. Good natured, sporty, good with children, and an excellent guard.

Origin: Named after the valley of Aire in Yorkshire. Formerly called the Waterside Terrier and originally kept by Yorkshire gamekeepers to keep down vermin. It is believed that the Airedale was crossed with the Otterhound. Used extensively as a guard prior to World War I when the German Shepherd predominated in this role. Many believe that the Airedale's guarding abilities are superior. It can also be trained to the gun.

Grooming: Daily brushing, using a stiff brush. The coat should be hand stripped, if you intend to exhibit. Clipping will spoil it for show purposes.

Exercising: Revels in its freedom but, despite its size, will adapt to living in an average-sized home.

Colouring: Body, top of neck and top surface of tail saddle black or grizzle; remainder tan.

Desired qualities: The Airedale has a hard, dense and wiry coat, 'V' shaped ears, dark eyes that are small but not prominent, and a short, strong, straight and level back.

Drawbacks: Terrier-like, it is not averse to a scrap with its fellows.

American Cocker Spaniel

Characteristics: Glamorous and obedient small spaniel that makes an excellent family pet and will also satisfy the sportsman in the family, as it can be trained both to flush and to retrieve.

Origin: The American Cocker originated from Britain but was developed along different lines from the English Cocker. It is a smaller dog and has a much longer coat with well feathered forelegs, body and hindlegs above hocks.

Grooming: Needs daily brushing and combing and fairly skilled trimming. Best to seek advice from breeder, especially if it is the owner's intention to exhibit.

Exercising: Will benefit from plenty of exercise.

Colouring: Various. In self-colours no white allowed except on chest.

Desired qualities: An ever-wagging tail.

Drawbacks: Needs lots of grooming; and plenty of exercise if it is to keep its figure.

Australian Terrier

Characteristics: Sturdy, low-set dog, which resembles a Yorkshire Terrier. Brave, hardy and a kind protector of adults and children.

Origin: The breed evolved from various British terriers which arrived in Australia with early settlers. Indeed it is not surprising that it is sometimes mistaken for a Yorkshire Terrier because it is believed to have derived from the progeny of a 'Yorkie' bitch smuggled into Australia in a lady's muff and subsequently mated to a Cairn-like terrier.

Grooming: Use a bristle brush. Bathe a fortnight before a show.

Exercising: Terrier-like it enjoys being 'on the go', but adapts to life in the average sized home.

Colouring: Blue, steel-blue, or dark grey-blue with rich tan (not sandy) on face, ears, underbody, lower legs and feet, and around the vent (puppies excepted).

Desired qualities: Head long with flat skull of moderate width, full between eyes, with slight but definite stop. Movement should be free, springy and forceful.

Drawbacks: None known – a first class little companion and watch dog!

Basenji

Characteristics: Delightful, dignified, barkless dog from the Congo. It is gentle, affectionate and utterly devoted to its owner. Has an affinity with horses.

Origin: This is another breed whose likeness has been depicted on the tombs of the Pharoahs. It had however almost disappeared from sight until in the mid-nineteenth century, explorers in the Congo and southern Sudan found some breed members. It is a hunter of game and *Basenji* is a native word meaning 'Bush thing'.

Grooming: Use of hand glove. However this is a dog that will keep itself clean.

Exercising: Not ideally suited to town life, but will adapt to its owners' exercise capabilities.

Colouring: Pure black and white; red and white; black, tan and white with tan melon pips and mask; black, tan and white. The white should be on feet, chest and tail tips. White legs, blaze and white collar optional.

Desired qualities: Lightly built, finely boned aristocractic-looking animal, high on leg compared with length.

Drawbacks: Slightly aloof with strangers.

Basset Hound

Characteristics: Ideal family pet, but in fact a hound of ancient lineage, capable of great endurance in the field. Good with children.

Origin: Of French origin, the Basset is derived from the French Basset Artesian Normand, which was imported to England and crossed with the Bloodhound. Mainly kept as a pet nowadays, but still used to hunt hare.

Grooming: Brush and comb daily. Use a hound glove too.

Exercising: A scent hound that revels in exercise.

Colouring: Generally black, white and tan (tri-colour); lemon and white (bi-colour). But any recognised hound colour is accepted.

Desired qualities: Short legs. A certain amount of loose skin.

Drawbacks: Make sure you have good fencing. This breed will wander.

Beagle

Characteristics: A healthy, merry, smart little dog that adores children and makes a good show dog.

Origin: Mentioned in writings dating from 1475. Used to hunt hare in Britain for centuries and imported into the United States for that purpose. Hunts other quarries in different countries of the world, including jackal, wild pig and deer. Used as a gundog in Canada.

Grooming: Needs little grooming. Use a hound glove if you wish.

Exercising: Needs plenty.

Colouring: Any recognised hound colour except liver. Tip of stern, white.

Desired qualities: A sturdy, compactly built hound, its breed standard calling for the impression of quality without coarseness.

Drawbacks: Lovable, but determined. Not the ideal candidate for an obedience class and, hound-like, has a propensity to wander.

Bearded Collie

Characteristics: An alert, lively dog, not unlike a small Old English sheepdog. Loves children, and makes a devoted, trainable pet.

Origin: A long-standing herding dog in Scotland, but thought to be of Polish origin. Legend has it that, on a trading voyage to Scotland in 1514, three Polish Lowland Sheepdogs, two bitches and a dog, were swapped for a ram and a ewe. The breed has also been credited with Hungarian blood.

Grooming: Daily brushing. Beardies are popular show dogs. If you intend to exhibit, bathing and chalking are necessary.

Exercising: A working dog that needs plenty of exercise.

Colouring: Slate grey, reddish fawn, black, blue, all shades of grey, brown and sandy with and without white markings.

Desired qualities: This dog's bright, enquiring expression is one of its most distinctive features.

Drawbacks: None known.

Bedlington Terrier

Characteristics: An intelligent, game little dog that resembles both a shorn lamb and a miniature poodle. It is loving and easy to train.

Origin: It is known that a similar strain of terriers existed in the eighteenth century in Rothbury Forest, Northumberland (Northumbria). The Greyhound, Whippet, and Dandie Dinmont have been credited with playing a part in its makeup. The Bedlington Terrier Club was formed in 1875.

Grooming: This breed is excellent for asthmatics because its coat does not shed. Brush daily with a stiff brush and have the coat regularly trimmed.

Exercising: It is a terrier and, therefore, lively. It enjoys daily walks, but is adaptable to apartment living.

Colouring: Blue, liver or sandy with or without tan. Darker pigment to be encouraged.

Desired qualities: A graceful, lithe, muscular dog with a mild and gentle expression when in repose.

Drawbacks: Enjoys a scrap.

Belgian Shepherd Dog

Characteristics: Strong and intelligent guard that is faithful and affectionate, but needs firm, kindly handling, and is best suited to country life.

Origin: In 1891, a selection of shepherd dogs in various shapes and sizes were gathered at Brussels Veterinary University. It was decided to recognise three as Belgian Shepherd Dogs. Today there are in fact four: the Groenendael (long-coated black), the Tervueren (long-coated other than black), the Malinois (smooth-coated) and the Laekenois, (wire-coated).

Grooming: Little grooming other than routine brushing.

Exercising: Needs plenty and should do well in obedience work.

Colouring: Tervueren (as illustrated). All shades of red, fawn, grey with black overlay.

Desired qualities: Fine proportions and proud carriage of head, conveying an impression of graceful strength. Not only a sheepdog but a guard dog.

Drawbacks: Somewhat wary of strangers.

21

Bernese Mountain Dog

Characteristics: Gentle and beautiful Swiss mountain dog that is usually good with children, easily trained and makes an excellent pet, show and carting dog.

Origin: Of the four Swiss mountain dogs the Bernese is the best known internationally – the others are the Great Swiss Sennenhund, the Appenzell Sennenhund and the Entlebuch Sennenhund. Traditionally used to pull the milk cart in its country of origin. Breed members in the UK often pull little carts to raise funds at charity events. The St. Bernard and Newfoundland had a hand in its makeup.

Grooming: Daily brushing.

Exercising: Needs plenty.

Colouring: Jet black, with rich reddish brown on cheeks, over eyes, on all four legs and on chest.

Desired qualities: Strong, sturdy working dog. Active, alert, well boned and of striking colour.

Drawbacks: None known, but not ideally suited to suburbia.

Bichon Frisé

Characteristics: An elegant, powder-puff-like dog
resembling a poodle. It is intelligent and lively
with a friendly, outgoing nature.

Origin: A descendant of the Barbet (Water
Spaniel), its original name Barbichon was
shortened to its present form. Introduced into
the Canary Islands by sailors, prior to the
fourteenth century, it became the favourite of
the French and Spanish aristocracies and
appeared in a number of paintings by the
Spanish artist, Francisco de Goya (1746-1828).

Grooming: Don't contemplate buying a Bichon
unless you are a frustrated hair-dresser. It
requires elaborate scissoring and trimming. Ask
the breeder to explain what is entailed.

Exercising: Enjoys a romp as much as other
breeds despite its elegant coiffure.

Colouring: White, but cream or apricot markings
acceptable up to eighteen months of age.

Desired qualities: A well balanced dog of smart
appearance with head carriage that is proud and
high.

Drawbacks: The amount of grooming required.

Bloodhound

Characteristics: Powerful hound and superlative tracker and trailer. Gentle nature. Makes a good pet for those with plenty of space.

Origin: One of the oldest, purest hound breeds. Believed to have come to Britain with William the Conqueror in 1066.

Grooming: Daily use of a hound glove.

Exercising: A great deal. Join the Bloodhound Club and have fun.

Colouring: Black and tan, liver and tan (red and tan) and red.

Desired qualities: A noble and dignified expression. Smooth, short, weatherproof coat.

Drawbacks: The sound of its baying, unless you have understanding neighbours.

Border Collie

Characteristics: Intelligent working dog. Ideal choice for anyone interested in competitive obedience.

Origin: A modern strain developed from the working collies of the Scottish, English and Welsh border counties. Still used extensively as a sheep-dog and unsurpassed in competitive obedience.

Grooming: A equine dandy brush is ideal.

Exercising: Needs plenty. It is wrong to coop this natural worker up in an apartment or suburban home.

Colouring: Variety of colours, but not predominantly white.

Desired qualities: A tenacious, hardworking sheepdog of great tractability.

Drawbacks: Its natural inclination to herd people as well as animals. Needs a job to do whether with sheep, or in the obedience/agility ring.

Border Terrier

Characteristics: Small, good natured working terrier that is game, spirited and intelligent.

Origin: Evolved in the nineteenth century in the border counties of England and Scotland. Still found in greater numbers in that region. It was designed to run with hounds and to bolt the fox from its lair.

Grooming: Simple daily grooming, but will need a trim, if you intend to exhibit.

Exercising: Can run with a horse and is in its element having plenty of exercise.

Colouring: Red, wheaten, grizzle and tan or blue and tan.

Desired qualities: Head like that of an otter, but moderately broad in the skull, with short strong muzzle. It should essentially look like a working terrier.

Drawbacks: It is unfair to keep a Border Terrier unless you can provide good country walks.

Borzoi

Characteristics: An aloof and beautiful coursing hound that also makes a good show dog. Faithful and intelligent.

Origin: A Russian breed, used for centuries by the Czars for hunting wolves. Has been crossed with sheepdogs and hounds to add strength. The present-day strain was developed by the Grand Duke Nicolai Nicholayevitch. Achieved notoriety in the early days of cinema when photographed with screen idols, such as the late Jean Harlow.

Grooming: Regular brushing.

Exercising: Needs a great deal – and well away from farm stock!

Colouring: Any colour acceptable.

Desired qualities: Well balanced, graceful aristocrat that is dignified and elegant.

Drawbacks: Needs space. Remember it is a natural hunter. Not always good with children.

Boxer

Characteristics: Lovable, clownish pet that is nonetheless a good guard. Adores children and is a firm family favourite, also a popular show dog.

Origin: Traces back to the Mollossus, Mastiff type. Indeed the Brabant bull-baiter from which the English Bulldog descends also had a hand in the Boxer's makeup.

Grooming: Daily brushing.

Exercising: A bundle of energy that needs plenty of exercise – and games.

Colouring: Fawn or brindle. White markings acceptable if they do not exceed one third of ground colour.

Desired qualities: Great nobility, smooth coat, medium size, square build, strong bone and evident, well developed muscles.

Drawbacks: Powerful to hold, and not averse to a scrap – which it is likely to win.

Briard

Characteristics: Large and attractive French sheepdog that makes an excellent pet, guard and show dog.

Origin: Arguably better known that another French sheepdog, the Pyrenean Mountain Dog. (The other two, the Picardy and Beauceron are little seen outside their country of origin.) The Briard, which comes from the Brie area of France, has been known since the twelfth century and is known in its homeland as the *Berger* or *Chien de Brie*.

Grooming: Regular brushing. This dog generally keeps itself clean, despite its long coat.

Exercising: A working breed that needs plenty of exercise.

Colouring: All black, or with white hairs scattered through black coat. Fawn in all its shades; darker shades preferred.

Desired qualities: Rugged appearance, supple, muscular and well proportioned.

Drawbacks: None known.

Brittany

Characteristics: Energetic hunt-point retriever (formerly known as the Brittany Spaniel). It is a tireless, but affectionate and sensitive dog that is eager to please and responds to kind handling.

Origin: It is said that an Irish red and white setter, belonging to a Breton Count, mated with a local bitch, thus starting the breed; others say that it originated in Spain, or in the Argoat Forests of Brittany.

Grooming: Daily brushing.

Exercising: Needs plenty.

Colouring: Orange/white, liver/white, black/white or roan, or any of these colours in tri-colour.

Desired qualities: A spaniel-pointer that is small, compact, lively and squarely built.

Drawbacks: None known, but take care not to wound its feelings.

Bulldog

Characteristics: A brave, intelligent dog that, despite its somewhat fierce appearance, is good natured and adores children.

Origin: Undoubtedly descended from the fighting dogs of Ancient Rome, sharing ancestry with the Mastiff and Boxer.

Grooming: Use a stiff brush for daily grooming. Rub down with a hound glove, or piece of towelling.

Exercising: Regular, but fairly limited exercise. *Do not take out in hot weather.*

Colouring: Whole or smut (i.e. whole colour with black mask or muzzle).

Desired qualities: Smooth coated dog, thick set, rather low in stature, broad, powerful and compact.

Drawbacks: A delightful pet that unfortunately does not have a long lifespan, and cannot cope with strenuous exercise. An ideal pet for an elderly gentleman.

Bull Terrier

Characteristics: Known as the gladiator of the canine race. Strong, hardy and the picture of beauty – or ugliness – according to taste. It is affectionate and surprisingly gentle with children.

Origin: Undoubtedly began life as a fighting dog until this 'sport' was outlawed in Britain in 1835. The more equable temperament of today's English Bull Terrier is due, in some measure, to the efforts of James Hinks of Birmingham, England, who crossed a Bulldog and Dalmatian with a white English Terrier. Coloured Bull Terriers did not appear until after World War II.

Grooming: Daily brushing. Rub down with a piece of towelling.

Exercising: Enjoys – and needs – plenty. Best kept in the country.

Colouring: White, with pure white coat, or, if coloured, brindle preferred. Black brindle, red, fawn and tri-colour acceptable.

Desired qualities: A strongly built muscular dog that is well balanced and active with a keen, determined and intelligent expression.

Drawbacks: Not really a beginner's dog. Takes a bit of holding. You either love them or hate them.

Cairn Terrier

Characteristics: Happy, hardy family pet that is
  adaptable and intelligent. Has weather-resistant
  coat.

Origin: The oldest known strain of Cairn Terriers
  traces back to those founded by the late Captain
  MacLeod of Drynoch in the Isle of Skye, more
  than 150 years ago. In those days they were
  known as Shorthaired Skye Terriers. However,
  working terriers of the same type obviously
  existed in Scotland more than 300 years ago
  when King James VI of Scotland (King James I
  of England) ordered from Edinburgh, 'half a
  dozen earth dogs or terrieres' to be sent as a gift
  to France. These are thought to have been Cairn
  Terriers. *Cairn* is the Gaelic word for a pile of
  stones, an apt name for a terrier that 'goes to
  ground'.

Grooming: Brushing and combing. Nothing
  elaborate required.

Exercising: Has lots of energy.

Colouring: Cream, wheaten, red, grey or nearly
  black. Brindling in all these colours is
  acceptable.

Desired qualities: Agile and alert terrier of
  workmanlike, natural appearance.

Drawbacks: Can be a trifle nippy if unchecked.

Cavalier King Charles Spaniel

Characteristics: The largest of the toy breeds and
one of the most popular pet dogs in the United
Kingdom. It is hardy, good natured and almost
always good with children, and other pets.

Origin: Originates from the same stock as the
King Charles Spaniel, which is smaller and has
an apple-domed head. Traces back to Japan in
2000BC. Became popular at the English court in
the 1600s. The Cavalier was the original. The
King Charles evolved when shorter-nosed dogs
became the rage.

Grooming: Daily use of a bristle brush.

Exercising: Needs its daily walk, but will adapt to
your exercise capabilities.

Colouring: Black and tan, ruby, blenheim, tri-
colour.

Desired qualities: An active, graceful and well
balanced dog with gentle expression.

Drawbacks: None known.

Chihuahua (Longcoat)

Characteristics: Credited with being the world's
smallest dog (between 0.9 and 2.7 kg), the
Chihuahua is keenly intelligent, fiercely
protective and cheap to keep. Inordinately
affectionate.

Origin: Named after the State of Chihuahua,
Mexico, and believed to have been the sacred dog
of the Incas. Its ancestors trace to a larger dog,
the Techichi, kept by the Toltecs as early as the
ninth century AD.

Grooming: Use of soft brush. Rub the coat with a
velvet pad to add shine. Eye wipes will prevent
tear stains.

Exercising: Despite their reputation as lap dogs,
Chihuahuas enjoy a walk, but take care not to
overtire them.

Colouring: Any colour allowed – and there are
many to choose from.

Desired qualities: An alert, swift-moving little
dog with a saucy expression. A well rounded,
apple-domed skull is prized.

Drawbacks: The breed's inclination to take on all
comers regardless of size!

Chihuahua (Smooth-Coat)

Characteristics: Reckoned to be the smallest dog in the world, but there is a lot of size variance in pet specimens. Loving, strong-willed, first class guard dogs in miniature. Supremely intelligent.

Origin: Believed to have been the sacred dog of the Incas and still to be found in their native Mexico. Originally lived in holes in the ground, and still like the security of a box or some such hideaway.

Grooming: Use of a soft brush. The coat will gleam if rubbed down with a velvet pad or silk handkerchief. Stroking improves the coat.

Exercising: Despite the idea that you carry a Chihuahua in a shopping bag they do enjoy a walk and will toddle as far as most pet owners would wish. Don't overtire them, however, especially in the case of very tiny, and older, specimens.

Colouring: Any colour, or mixture of colours.

Desired qualities: An alert little dog, swift moving with brisk, forceful action and saucy expression.

Drawbacks: Can be a trifle foolhardy when confronted by larger, stronger breeds. Regular heart checks are recommended after middle age.

Chinese Crested Dog (Hairless)

Characteristics: Active, loving, gentle and exceedingly greedy. Very amusing, but not particularly intelligent.

Origin: Said to have arrived in South America via Chinese sailing ships many centuries ago, but possibly the result of mating the Mexican hairless dog (Xolocuintlis) and the Chihuahua. Certainly a mating between these two breeds produces a hairless dog, as has been proved.

Grooming: Regular bathing; also creaming, or oiling to keep skin smooth and supple. Any odd, straggly hairs are removed prior to exhibition. Care has to be taken to avoid sunburn in hot weather.

Colouring: Any colour or combination of colours.

Desired qualities: A small, active and graceful dog, medium to fine boned with a smooth, hairless body, with hair on feet, head and tail.

Drawbacks: Greed. Hyper-activity. Great fun, but not recommended for the obedience ring.

NB The Chinese Crested Powder Puff is a haired variety like a small, long-haired sheepdog.

Chow Chow

Characteristics: Beautiful, odour-free dog, which in common with small bears, has a black tongue. It is exceedingly loyal but strong-willed, and needs firm but gentle handling.

Origin: The Chow Chow – the name derives from the Chinese Choo Hunting Dog –i s reputed to be the original Lama's Mastiff and is one of the oldest members of the Spitz family. Its flesh is a delicacy in many parts of Asia, where it is also prized for its fur and as a hunter of game.

Grooming: Use of wire brush. A few minutes' brushing daily (with a longer session at weekends) should keep the Chow Chow's coat gleaming.

Exercising: Adaptable to town or country, but relishes outdoor life.

Colouring: Whole coloured black, red, blue, fawn, cream or white, frequently shaded, but not in patches or parti-coloured (underpart of tip of tail and back of thighs are often of a lighter shade).

Desired qualities: An active, compact, short-coupled and well balanced dog, well knit in frame, with tail carried over back.

Drawbacks: A fierce opponent if provoked.

Clumber Spaniel

Characteristics: Impressive, heavily built spaniel, of good temperament and keen intelligence. Makes a good family pet, but most Clumbers enjoy the life of a sporting dog, which is the role for which they were bred.

Origin: The Clumber, the result of crossing the Basset Hound with the now-extinct Alpine Spaniel, was developed by the French Duc de Noailles prior to the Revolution. Sadly, the Duke was killed in the hostilities, but he had already entrusted his dogs to the Duke of Newcastle at Clumber Park, after which the breed was to take its name.

Grooming: Regular brushing.

Exercising: A working dog that, despite its weight, excels as a beater and retriever.

Colouring: Plain white body preferred with lemon markings; orange permissible. Slight head markings and freckled muzzle.

Desired qualities: Well balanced, heavily boned dog with a thoughtful expression.

Drawbacks: None known. It is slow, but sure, and utterly reliable.

Cocker Spaniel (English Cocker Spaniel)

Characteristics: The 'Merry Cocker' is happy and long-lived. It will admirably combine the roles of family pet and gun dog. Will both flush and retrieve.

Origin: Not really a British dog at all, but of Spanish origin, hence the word 'spaniel'. However, the word 'cocker' was included because of the dog's ability to flush out woodcock. Its lineage traces back to the fourteenth century.

Grooming: Regular brushing. Care has to be taken that the ears do not become tangled – or drop into the food bowl.

Exercising: Needs plenty. This breed has a tendency to become overweight, if it is over-fed and/or under-exercised.

Colouring: Various. In self-colours no white allowed except on chest.

Desired qualities: Merry nature with ever-wagging tail.

Drawbacks: None known.

Dachsund (Teckel)

Characteristics: Affectionate, courageous and
intelligent. Good watchdogs, usually fond of
children, and with a great sense of fun. There are
three varieties to choose from: smooth-haired,
long-haired and wire-haired, each of which has a
miniature version.

Origin: Bred as a badger hound in Germany and
still loves to dig up the garden! They were derived
from the old German hunting dog, the Bibarhund.
However, the wire-hair was introduced by crossing
the smooth with the Dandie Dinmont, the long-
hair by crossing the smooth with the Stoberhund
(a German gundog) and a spaniel.

Grooming: Use of stiff brush on the long-hair and
wire-hair, a hound glove and silk handkerchief, or
soft brush, on the smooth.

Exercising: Enjoys a good walk, but please don't let
your Dachsie jump up on furniture – or on walls
or stiles on country walks – they are prone to back
trouble!

Colouring: All colours allowed (except white), and
in dapples, which should be evenly marked all
over.

Desired qualities: A dog that is long and low, but
with a compact, well muscled body, a bold, defiant
carriage of head and an intelligent expression.

Drawbacks: Loud bark (which could be an asset in
small watchdog). Sometimes shows slight
aggression towards strangers.

41

Dalmatian

Characteristics: A most attractive, good-natured dog, that is generally long-lived and makes a loyal, trainable pet.

Origin: Generally thought of as a British carriage dog but in fact originated in Yugoslavia. Found renewed and continuing fame in 1959 following the release of the film, *A Hundred and One Dalmatians,* the Walt Disney production based on Dodie Smith's book. Also a popular show dog, although the variety has not achieved a Best in Show at Crufts since 1978.

Grooming: Daily brush and rub down.

Exercising: Needs plenty. Will keep pace with a horse.

Colouring: Ground colour pure white, with dense black or liver brown spots. The spots should be one-penny to fifty-pence coin-sized, and should not run together, but be round and well defined.

Desired qualities: A distinctively spotted dog, balanced, strong, muscular and active.

Drawbacks: Fairly exuberant. Watch out for that coat, if you are houseproud. It sheds!

Dandie Dinmont

Characteristics: Smart, distinctive terrier, that is good with children and has many uses ranging from show dog to little guard.

Origin: Dandie Dinmonts trace back to a character by name of Piper Allan who kept two Dandies named Charlie and Peachem in the 1700s. However, it was another fancier of 'pepper and mustard' terriers who sold a specimen or two to the Scottish novelist, Sir Walter Scott. Thereafter, the breed was named after a character in Sir Walter's novel, *Guy Mannering*.

Grooming: Stiff brush and comb. Needs hand-stripping for exhibition. Best to obtain advice from breeder.

Exercising: Will adapt to suburban living, but given their original popularity as fox and badger hunters, it is not surprising that they thrive best if given plenty of exercise.

Colouring: Pepper and mustard.

Desired qualities: A game, workmanlike terrier with a distinctive head, a beautiful, silky covering and large, wise, intelligent eyes.

Drawbacks: Tends to be a one-person dog. A trifle suspicious of strangers.

Deerhound

Characteristics: Graceful and hardy. Still used for coursing but nowadays kept mainly as a faithful pet by those with the room to accommodate it and the energy to exercise it.

Origin: The Deerhound is the breed chosen as the emblem of the Scottish Kennel Club and, like the Dandie Dinmont, it was a favourite of the novelist, Sir Walter Scott. It was purpose-bred for hunting, but with the advent of breech-loading rifles was no longer needed in this role, becoming instead a delightful pet.

Grooming: Has weather-resistant coat and needs little attention other than brushing and the removal of shaggy hairs.

Exercising: The Deerhound, which can live indoors or in an outside kennel, needs a great deal of exercise.

Colouring: Dark blue grey, darker and lighter greys or brindles and yellows, sandy-red or red fawns with black points.

Desired qualities: A dog that resembles a Rough-coated Greyhound of larger size and bone.

Drawbacks: Make sure it is well trained if you live in sheep country!

Doberman

Characteristics: An aloof, brave guard that makes a faithful pet if selected from good stock and carefully trained.

Origin: Designed by Louis Dobermann of Apolda in Thuringia, Germany. Herr Dobermann, a tax collector, wanted a fierce dog to accompany him on his rounds. He chose the German Pinscher for aggression and alertness, the Rottweiler for its stamina and tracking ability and the Manchester Terrier, to which the Doberman obviously owes much of its outward appearance. Pointer may also have been added.

Grooming: Brushing and a daily rub-down with towelling.

Exercising: Needs plenty. Like the German Shepherd Dog, this natural guard is always 'on duty'.

Colouring: Definite black, brown, blue or fawn (Isabella) only with rust red markings.

Desired qualities: A medium sized dog that is muscular and elegant with well set body. It should be bold and alert. Shyness or viciousness are very highly undesirable.

Drawbacks: Needs firm but kind training.

Elkhound

Characteristics: A hardy, hunting Spitz with bold, energetic disposition. It is intelligent and usually good with children.

Origin: Has existed in its native Norway for many centuries. Its task was to go elk-hunting with its master and hold the prey at bay until he moved in for the kill.

Grooming: Brush and comb daily.

Exercising: Needs plenty.

Colouring: Grey, of various shades.

Desired qualities: The Elkhound should have a powerful, compact body; square outline and proud carriage. The tail should be tightly curled over its back, a characteristic of the Spitz breeds.

Drawbacks: None known, although firm but gentle discipline is needed in early life.

English Setter

Characteristics: A beautiful dog that can ideally combine the roles of family pet and gundog. Good with children.

Origin: Most breed historians refer to Edward Laverack (1815-1877) for information on this breed. In Laverack's book, *The Setter,* he refers to the breed as 'but a spaniel improved'. It was Laverack who through interbreeding brought about the English setter on which the present standard was based.

Grooming: Use a stiff brush and a steel comb. If you plan to exhibit, any straggly hairs will need to be removed. There are some differences between the American and British exhibition standards.

Exercising: Needs plenty.

Colouring: Black and white (blue belton), orange and white (orange belton), lemon and white (lemon belton), liver and white (liver belton) or tri-colour.

Desired qualities: A dog of medium height, clean in outline, elegant in appearance and movement.

Drawbacks: None known, except perhaps that it usually does not like its own company.

English Springer Spaniel

Characteristics: An attractive and intelligent spaniel that admirably combines the role of family pet and gundog. It is unusual to find one of bad temperament. Good with children.

Origin: Ranks with the Clumber as one of the oldest 'British' spaniels, and is a great favourite with the sportsman as a gundog. May have originally been called the Norfolk Spaniel. The word 'springer' comes from the dog's task of springing game for the hunter.

Grooming: Daily brushing. Alas, this breed is renowned for bringing mud into the house, and shaking itself when it comes in out of the rain.

Exercising: Best suited to country life.

Colouring: Liver and white, black and white, or either of these colours with tan markings.

Desired qualities: Symmetrically built, compact, strong, merry, active. Highest on leg, and raciest in build, of all British land spaniels.

Drawbacks: None known. But don't under-exercise; otherwise, like the Cocker, it could lose its figure. Also remember it has a tendency to shake itself when coming in out of the rain.

Field Spaniel

Characteristics: Docile and attractive spaniel that ideally combines the role of family pet and sportsman's dog. It is good with children, and of excellent temperament. Alas, it is all too rarely seen.

Origin: The Field Spaniel developed along the same lines as the Cocker until, in 1892, they were separately classified. The Field Spaniel was, at one time, in danger of extinction, but fortunately the Field Spaniel Society, which was reformed in 1948, is a band of keen devotees who are doing all they can to preserve this fine spaniel.

Grooming: Daily brushing and combing.

Exercising: Best suited to country life.

Colouring: Black, liver or roan. Any one of these with tan markings.

Desired qualities: Well balanced, noble, upstanding sporting spaniel, built for activity and endurance.

Drawbacks: None known.

Finnish Spitz

Characteristics: Brave, faithful and intelligent. A hunting dog that nevertheless, makes a fine housepet and is usually good with children.

Origin: The national dog of Finland. It has been popular in Scandinavia for some years and, in recent times, has won many devotees in Britain both as pet and show dog. It was originally bred as a 'bird' dog.

Grooming: Daily brushing.

Exercising: Not a kennel dog. All the same it does enjoy a run in the fresh air.

Colouring: On back, reddish-brown or red gold, preferably bright. Hairs on inner sides of ears, cheeks, under muzzle, on breast, abdomen, behind shoulders, inside legs, backs of thighs and underside of tail are of lighter shades.

Desired qualities: The whole appearance of this dog should indicate liveliness. A compact, hard-conditioned hunting dog with medium bone.

Drawbacks: None known.

Flat-Coated Retriever

Characteristics: Natural retriever and first class guard. Makes a good housepet and is reliable with children. Also popular in the show ring.

Origin: Probably evolved from the crossing of the Labrador Retriever with the Collie and spaniels. Has not suffered from the over-popularity of the former breeds.

Grooming: Daily brushing.

Exercising: Needs plenty. Enjoys picking up.

Colouring: Black or liver only.

Desired qualities: Generously endowed with gundog ability. Medium-sized, showing power without lumber, and raciness without weediness.

Drawbacks: None known.

French Bulldog

Characteristics: Courageous dog, with clown-like qualities. Bat ears and short, undocked tail are essential features of the breed. Affectionate and devoted, it loves human company and gets on with other pets.

Origin: The French are credited with the development of the breed. It is uncertain whether 'Frenchies' derive from small English Bulldogs taken to France by Nottingham laceworkers in the nineteenth century, or from crossings with dogs imported to France from Spain, but they are obviously the descendants of small Bulldogs.

Grooming: One of the easiest dogs to prepare for exhibition. Brush daily with a stiff brush and rub down coat with a towel. Lubricate facial creases to prevent soreness.

Exercising: Enjoy moderate exercise, but never, in common with other flat-nosed breeds, in hot weather.

Colouring: The colours allowed are brindle, pied and fawn.

Desired qualities: Head massive, square and broad. Skull nearly flat between ears, with a domed forehead, the loose skin forming symmetrical wrinkles.

Drawbacks: Might be a trifle heavy (12.7 kg/28 lbs) for folk wanting a small breed that they can lift in and out of a car, or onto the show table.

German Shepherd Dog (Alsatian)

Characteristics: Intelligent, faithful, and a first class guard. Likes a job of work to do.

Origin: As early as the seventh century AD, a dog resembling the German Shepherd, but with a lighter coat, existed in its native Germany. By the sixteenth century, the coat had considerably darkened. It was in 1882, in Hanover, that the breed was first exhibited at a dog show. Introduced into Britain after World War I, the GSD, as devotees call it, was officially known until 1971 as the Alsatian. In that year the original name, German Shepherd Dog, was restored.

Grooming: Daily brushing.

Exercising: Needs plenty. Best if given a task to perform, whether as a guard, working in agility or obedience, or as a guide dog for the blind or assistance dog for the disabled.

Colouring: Black or black saddle with tan, or gold to light grey markings. All black, all grey, or grey with lighter or brown markings referred to as Sables.

Desired qualities: A versatile working dog that is tireless, and has keen scenting ability.

Drawbacks: Tendency to overguard.

53

German Short-Haired Pointer

Characteristics: An obedient, affectionate
gundog that admirably combines the roles of
family pet and sporting dog.

Origin: The German Short-Haired Pointer is in
fact of Spanish origin, deriving from dogs
imported into Germany and crossed with the
English Foxhound and other hounds to provide
speed and scenting ability. English Pointer blood
was also added.

Grooming: Regular brushing.

Exercising: Needs plenty.

Colouring: Solid liver, liver and white spotted and
ticked, liver and white ticked, solid black or
black and white in the same variations (not tri-
colour).

Desired qualities: A noble, steady dog, showing
power, endurance and speed.

Drawbacks: None, but don't keep it cooped up all
day.

German Wire-Haired Pointer

Characteristics: An obedient, affectionate gundog that admirably combines the roles of family pet and gundog.

Origin: (See German short-haired pointer.) Similar background, but the wire coat was obviously derived from other German hunting dogs. It has been known in Germany since the Middle Ages.

Grooming: Regular brushing.

Exercising: Needs plenty.

Colouring: Liver and white, solid liver, black and white.

Desired qualities: Medium sized hunting dog with wire hair completely covering skin.

Drawbacks: None, but don't keep it cooped up all day.

Golden Retriever

Characteristics: Beautiful and intelligent gundog that is good with children, makes a fine show dog and admirably combines the roles of a sportsman's dog and family pet.

Origin: Despite hints of Russian ancestry, it is generally accepted that the Golden first saw the light of day on a Scottish estate in a litter born of retriever and spaniel ancestry.

Grooming: Brushing daily.

Exercising: Needs plenty.

Colouring: Any shade of gold or cream.

Desired qualities: Symmetrical, balanced, active, powerful level mover, sound with kindly expression.

Drawbacks: None known. A sound choice.

NB The Golden's flat or wavy coat is not to be confused with the short, dense one of the Labrador Retriever.

Gordon Setter

Characteristics: Fine, stylish Scottish gundog. A tireless worker that admirably combines the roles of family pet and sportsman's dog. Good with children.

Origin: This, the only native Scottish gundog, was bred at Gordon Castle, Banffshire, the seat of the Duke of Richmond and Gordon. The breed was established by the 4th Duke in the late 1770s, and it is likely that Collie and Bloodhound were used in its makeup.

Grooming: Regular brushing.

Exercising: Needs plenty.

Colouring: Deep shining coal black, without rustiness, with markings of chestnut red, i.e. lustrous tan.

Desired qualities: A medium-sized dog of distinguished appearance, robust and medium-boned. Its head should be lean and noble.

Drawbacks: Don't buy a setter if you want a guard dog. It is likely to love visitors to death.

Great Dane

Characteristics: The Apollo of the dog world. Strong and devoted, it usually gets on well with children and other animals.

Origin: An ancient breed and a likely descendant of the Molossus Hounds of ancient Rome. Bismarck aroused interest in the breed when, by crossing the Great Dane with the Mastiff of southern Germany, he brought about a Dane type similar to that which we know today.

Grooming: Use a body brush. Despite its size this dog does better when kept indoors and will settle down happily in a warm corner.

Exercising: Needs plenty.

Colouring: Brindle, fawn, blue, black and harlequin.

Desired qualities: Very muscular, strongly but elegantly built, with look of dash and daring, of being ready to go anywhere and do anything.

Drawbacks: Does not have a lengthy lifespan, eight or nine years being average.

Griffon Bruxellois and Petit Brabançon

Characteristics: Delightful, terrier-like toy breed, with a monkey face, strong will, and loving nature. There are two varieties, rough- and smooth-coated, the latter being called the Petit Brabançon.

Origin: Probably derives from the Affenpinscher with an infusion of Pug blood. The Pug is doubtless responsible for the smooth-coated variety. A Belgian breed long used to keep down vermin in stable yards and sometimes referred to as the mongrel of the pure-bred dog world, this charming little fellow rose in the world when the late Queen Astrid of Belgium took a fancy to it and greatly popularised the breed, which now has an enthusiastic international following.

Grooming: The smooth coat needs brushing and a rub-down with towelling. The rough-coat has to be hand-stripped twice a year. It is not an easy breed to prepare for the show ring. Best to seek advice from breeder.

Colouring: Clear red, black or black and rich tan without white markings. Ideally each hair should be an even red from tip to root.

Desired qualities: Well balanced, square little dog, giving the appearance of measuring the same from withers to tail root as from withers to ground.

Drawbacks: Does sometimes enjoy a scrap with its canine fellows.

Hamiltonstovare (Hamilton Hound)

Characteristics: Hardy and sound scent hound that makes an affectionate, intelligent family dog.

Origin: This Swedish hound was named after its creator, Count Hamilton, the founder of the Swedish Kennel Club. The Count designed the Hamiltonstovare by crossing the English Foxhound with, among others, the German Holstein Hound and the Hanoverian Haidbracke. Unlike English Foxhounds, which live in packs, this hound resides with its owner.

Grooming: Regular use of a hound glove.

Exercising: Plenty.

Colouring: Upper side of neck, back, sides of trunk and upper side of tail black. Head and legs, side of neck, trunk and tail brown. White blaze on upper part of muzzle, underside of neck, breast, tip of tail and feet.

Desired qualities: Well proportioned, tri-coloured hound giving impression of great strength and stamina.

Drawbacks: The neighbours might object to its baying.

Hungarian Puli

Characteristics: An unusual, loyal and intelligent guard, with a corded, water-resistant coat.

Origin: The best known of the Hungarian sheep-dogs, perhaps because of its unusual tactic of jumping on the backs of the sheep in order to direct them. It has been around for 1,000 years or more and is a descendant of sheepdogs which arrived in Hungary with the Magyars.

Grooming: This dog, with its long, black cords, or ringlets, has a naturally scruffy appearance. Each cord has to be separated by hand every day, and brushed.

Exercising: Prefers the country life and ample exercise, but is fairly adaptable.

Colouring: Black, rusty-black, white and various shades of grey and apricot.

Desired qualities: Sturdy, muscular and wiry, with fine bone. Whole well covered with long (according to age), profuse, corded coat.

Drawbacks: Not too keen on strangers.

Hungarian Vizla

Characteristics: First class Hungarian gundog. Ideally combines the roles of family pet and sportsman's pointer and retriever. Beautiful appearance. Sound temperament.

Origin: This is the national dog of Hungary and is said to have been developed by Magyar nobility. It is one of the world's purest breeds.

Grooming: Daily brushing.

Exercising: Needs plenty.

Colouring: Russet gold.

Desired qualities: Medium-sized, of distinguished appearance, robust and medium-boned.

Drawbacks: None known.

Ibizan Hound

Characteristics: Ancient, kindly gundog that admirably combines the role of hunter and family pet. In Britain it is kept mainly as a fairly rare and charming companion.

Origin: Like the Pharaoh Hound – which it resembles – the Ibizan Hound is similar to those dogs whose likenesses appear on rock stone and papyrus of ancient Egypt. Bones of dogs such as these date back to 4770 BC. When the Romans invaded Egypt the Carthaginians and Phoenicians fled to the Isle of Ibiza where they remained, with their hounds, for a century. The hounds were to remain there as a charming legacy.

Grooming: Regular brushing.

Exercising: Needs plenty of exercise. However, this is definitely not a breed to be kept in an outside kennel.

Colouring: Solid white, chestnut or lion, or any combination of these colours.

Desired qualities: Tall, narrow and finely built, with large, erect ears. Has the ability to jump great heights without take-off run!

Drawbacks: Acute hearing. Very sensitive. Hates to be shouted at.

Irish (Red) Setter/Irish (Red and White) Setter

Characteristics: Beautiful dog that is excellent with children and other animals, and has tireless energy. No good as a guard, though.

Origin: Frequently referred to as the Red Setter – indeed Irish Red and White setters are also now becoming popular – the Irish evolved out of crossings between the Irish Water Spaniel, the English and Gordon Setters and, it is believed, the Spanish Pointer.

Grooming: Regular brushing.

Exercising: Boundless energy. Seems to like running with horses.

Colouring: Rich chestnut. (The Irish Red and White is clearly parti-coloured, i.e. base colour pearl white, with solid red patches.)

Desired qualities: Racy, balanced and full of quality.

Drawbacks: Slow to mature, very energetic, demonstratively affectionate – no good for discouraging burglars.

Irish Water Spaniel

Characteristics: Attractive and unusual curly-coated spaniel, that is a powerful swimmer, versatile gundog, and devoted companion.

Origin: Developed in Ireland. Looks like a cross between a Standard Poodle and a spaniel, but though the former suggestion is unlikely, spaniels were definitely used in its makeup.

Grooming: Daily brushing, and some stripping. Best to check with breeder, especially if it is the intention to exhibit.

Exercising: Good all-round gundog, which particularly excels at wildfowling. Can be kept as a housepet but is not suited to suburban life.

Colouring: Rich dark liver with purplish tint, or bloom, peculiar to the breed and sometimes referred to as puce-liver.

Desired qualities: Smart, upstanding, strongly built, compact.

Drawbacks: None known, but best kept in the country.

Irish Wolfhound

Characteristics: A gentle giant, fierce only when provoked. Loves children and enjoys being a pet companion, provided that it has plenty of space.

Origin: The national dog of Ireland and a faithful, gentle protector despite its original role as a killer of wolves. It is thought to have come from Greece with the invading Celts, circa 279 BC. Of interest is that the breed standard for the Irish Wolfhound was in fact drawn up in 1885 by a Scots Army Captain, George Graham, who had spent twenty-three years rescuing the breed from extinction.

Grooming: Not difficult. Regular brushing and the removal of any straggly hairs.

Exercising: No more than average, but does need plenty of space in which to play.

Colouring: Grey, brindle, red, black, pure white, fawn, wheaten and steel grey.

Desired qualities: A dog of great size, symmetry, strength and commanding appearance. Very muscular yet gracefully built.

Drawbacks: Not suitable for the average, suburban home. And remember that a dog of this size is not cheap to keep.

Italian Short-Haired Segugio

Characteristics: Italian hunting dog of ancient origin, rarely seen in Britain, though a few are beginning to appear on the show scene. It is lively, courageous and extremely intelligent.

Origin: The short-haired Segugio (there is also a coarse-haired variety) has for centuries been unsurpassed as a hunter of game, particularly hare, and has an exceptional sense of smell. It is a descendant of the coarsing dogs of ancient Egypt, which arrived in Italy and were crossed with Mastiffs.

Grooming: Brushing. Use a hound glove.

Exercising: Needs plenty.

Colouring: Solid fawn from deep reddish fawn to very pale fawn; back and tan.

Desired qualities: Resonant voice, pleasant to listen to. Gallops at the hunt.

Drawbacks: None known. But a full and frank discussion with breeder is recommended.

Italian Spinone

Characteristics: An affectionate and attractive gundog that is loyal and easy to train.

Origin: Although usually thought of as an Italian gundog, the Spinone in fact originated in the French region of Bresse, later finding its way to Piedmont, Italy, where its ability to work in marshy, wooded country was much appreciated by the Italian aristocracy. It will both point and retrieve and is a loyal companion. The makeup of the Spinone is attributed to the French Griffon, the French and German Pointers, the Porcelaine Barbet and Korthals Griffon.

Grooming: Regular brushing.

Exercising: Needs plenty.

Colouring: White, white with orange markings, solid white peppered orange, white with brown markings, white speckled with brown (brown roan), with or without large brown markings.

Desired qualities: Solid and squarely built, strong-boned and well muscled. Kind and earnest expression. Tough, thick, slightly wiry, close-fitting coat.

Drawbacks: None known.

Jack Russell Terrier (Parson)

Characteristics: An affectionate, sporty terrier of great popularity. Good housedog, but best suited to a country home.

Origin: There has been such a variation in the size and coat texture of Jack Russells that the British Kennel Club would not grant a breed standard. In comparatively recent times, the Parson Jack Russell Club has been formed, and the breed is now being exhibited in the show ring. The variety traces back to the Reverend Jack Russell, a parson in Devonshire, England, who died more than 100 years ago. The sporting clergyman built up a strain of hunt terriers that would go to ground and bolt the fox. He was also a judge of terriers and an early member of the Kennel Club.

Grooming: Use a stiff brush.

Exercising: Jack Russells need plenty. Not really a good choice for the little old ladies who tend to acquire them.

Colouring: White, or white with tan, lemon or black markings.

Desired qualities: A game little working dog.

Drawbacks: Excitable in a pack.

Japanese Akita

Characteristics: Large and powerful Spitz variety that is intelligent, faithful, and a first class guard.

Origin: The national dog of Japan and a wild boar and deer hunter. Although of obvious Icelandic descent, it has been known in Japan's Akita province for more than 300 years. The Akita found its way to America after World War II, examples having been brought back by returning servicemen. More recently, it has had immense popularity in Britain, where it is drawing large entries in the show ring.

Grooming: Regular brushing.

Exercising: Needs plenty. It has great stamina.

Colouring: Any colour, including white, brindle or pinto.

Desired qualities: Large powerful dog, alert with much substance and heavy bone.

Drawbacks: Not really a beginner's dog, despite its generally good temperament.

Japanese Chin

Characteristics: Delightful toy-sized dog that is affectionate, loyal, and good with children.

Origin: Much like the Pekingese and possibly descended from similar stock, though it is taller than the Peke and has a lighter body. The Japanese Chin (or Spaniel) was revered by the Emperors of Japan for more than 10,000 years. It is said that some of these little dogs were kept in small cages, like oriental birds, though how this was possible I do not know. In any event, the breed is reckoned to have found its way to Europe, with seamen, in medieval times.

Grooming: Use a bristle brush.

Exercising: Will adapt to its owner's capabilities. Enjoys a game.

Colouring: Black and white or red and white. Red includes all shades of sable, lemon or orange.

Desired qualities: Elegant and aristocratic, smart, compact with profuse coat.

Drawbacks: As with other flat-nosed breeds, care must be taken that it is not over-exerted in warm weather. Never forget to take a supply of iced water with you when travelling with this little dog.

Japanese Spitz

Characteristics: A small Spitz that is affectionate and companionable, but somewhat chary of strangers. It is loyal and intelligent.

Origin: The Japanese Spitz, a close relation of the Norrbotten Spitz, has developed along separate lines in Japan, to which country it was imported many years ago. Until comparatively recently it was little known outside Japan, but there are now quite a few breed members in Britain. The breed is proving popular in the show ring.

Grooming: Regular brushing.

Exercising: It is only fair to give this herding dog a good amount of exercise. However, it will normally adapt to its owner's capabilities.

Colouring: Pure white.

Desired qualities: Profuse, pure white, stand-off coat. Pointed muzzle, triangular ears, standing erect. Tail curled over back, as is characteristic of the Spitz breeds.

Drawbacks: None, other than initial apprehension at meeting strangers.

Keeshond

Characteristics: Loyal dog of equable temperament. Lives long and makes an excellent pet.

Origin: The Keeshond is the national dog of Holland and originated as a barge dog. However, like other Spitz varieties its ancestry must trace back to the Arctic circle.

Grooming: This dog needs a lot of grooming, preferably using a stiff brush.

Exercising: Will adapt to its owner's capabilities.

Colouring: A mixture of grey and black. Undercoat very pale grey or cream (not tawny). All shades of grey acceptable, body hairs black tipped. Shoulder markings well defined and all markings definite. Forelegs and hocks cream with no black below wrist or hock. Pencilling acceptable.

Desired qualities: A sturdy, intelligent dog with a short, compact body and confident carriage.

Drawbacks: Rather noisy bark. Strong guarding instincts.

Labrador Retriever

Characteristics: Natural retriever and first class housedog. Good with children and makes a fine show dog. Also does well in obedience. Ideally combines the role of sportsman's dog and family pet.

Origin: Came to Britain with fishermen from Newfoundland in the 1830s. Its original task was to land the fishermen's nets. It is still a fine swimmer.

Grooming: Daily brushing.

Exercising: Needs plenty. Very exuberant in youth.

Colouring: Wholly black, yellow or liver/chocolate.

Desired qualities: Strongly built, short-coupled, very active, and broad in skull. Good tempered and agile.

Drawbacks: None known. Sound choice.

NB There is also the Curly Coated Retriever in whose makeup the Labrador Retriever and, probably, the Irish Water Spaniel played a part; also the Chesapeake Bay Retriever, a favourite in the USA, which has only recently found a band of devotees in Britain.

Lakeland Terrier

Characteristics: Attractive, medium-sized terrier, not unlike a small Airedale. It is affectionate and lively, and makes an excellent guard for the home.

Origin: Of Celtic origin and closely allied to the Welsh Terrier, both being descended from the old Black and Tan Terrier, the Airedale Terrier and the Fox Terrier.

Grooming: This is another breed that requires hand-stripping if you want to exhibit. No reason why it should not be clipped if the dog is destined just to be a house pet. Best to seek advice from breeder.

Exercising: Terrier-like, it has plenty of energy and appreciates good, long walks.

Colouring: Black and tan, blue and tan, red, wheaten, red grizzle, liver, blue or black.

Desired qualities: Smart, workmanlike terrier 'on the tip-toe of expectation'.

Drawbacks: None known.

Lancashire Heeler

Characteristics: Happy, affectionate little dog
that will work cattle and has strong terrier
instincts. Has only recently made its debut in
the British show ring.

Origin: Common for many years in north-west
England, where it would hunt rabbits, herd
cattle and dispose of small vermin, this breed
has only been granted a British Kennel Club
show standard in the past five years.

Grooming: Regular brushing.

Exercising: Boundless energy. Best suited to farm
life, or at any rate an owner who enjoys the great
outdoors.

Colouring: Black, with rich tan marking on
muzzle, spots on cheeks and often above eyes.

Desired qualities: Low-set, strong and active
worker.

Drawbacks: There are – as in the case of all
breeds – exceptions. However, the Heeler is not
altogether reliable with children and can be a
little snappy.

Lhasa Apso

Characteristics: Happy, confident little dog that is good with children and makes an excellent pet and show dog provided that you have plenty of time for grooming.

Origin: This dog has existed for centuries in the mountains of Tibet and was highly prized by the Dalai Lama, who would give choice specimens to visiting Chinese Emperors. Indeed it is likely that a crossing of the Lhasa Apso with the Chinese Pekingese created the very similar Shih Tzu (or Chrysanthemum Dog).

Grooming: Extensive brushing and combing.

Exercising: Despite its glamorous appearance, this is an active little dog that enjoys plenty of exercise.

Colouring: Golden, sandy, honey, dark grizzle, slate, smoke, parti-colour, black, white or brown.

Desired qualities: Well balanced, sturdy, heavy-coated.

Drawbacks: None known, but does need a fair amount of attention.

Lowchen (Little Lion Dog)

Characteristics: Unusual, happy, lively toy dog that is intelligent, generally healthy, and makes a good show dog.

Origin: Regarded as a French breed, but known in both France and Spain since the late 1500s, when it was much favoured by the beauteous Duchess of Alba, subject of paintings by the artist Francisco Goya, (1746-1828), in one of which a small dog, much like the Lowchen, is depicted. The Lowchen would appear to derive from the same stock as the Bichon Frisé, Maltese and Bichon Bolognese.

Grooming: The coat is clipped in traditional lion clip, the tail also clipped and topped with a plume, giving appearance of a little lion. Therefore, much advice is needed from breeder before purchase, especially if it is the intention to exhibit in the show ring.

Exercising: Will adapt to its owner's exercise capabilities.

Colouring: Any colour or combination of colours permissible.

Desired qualities: A happy, lively little dog that is strongly built, active and well balanced.

Drawbacks: None known.

Maltese

Characteristics: Very loving, usually long-lived little dog, reliable with children and generally healthy.

Origin: Arguably one of the oldest European toy breeds and usually associated with Malta, where it has been known for many centuries. It was known in Britain as early as the reign of King Henry VIII, when it was much favoured as a pet by the ladies of his court. The Maltese was exhibited in the British show ring as early as 1864.

Grooming: Daily brushing, using a bristle brush. This is not the easiest of breeds to prepare for exhibition, and advice from the breeder should be sought.

Exercising: Will adapt to its owner's exercise capabilities.

Colouring: Pure white, but light lemon markings permissible.

Desired qualities: Smart, white-coated dog, with proud head carriage.

Drawbacks: Rather sensitive. Thrives on affection.

Maremma Sheepdog

Characteristics: Beautiful Italian sheepdog of great intelligence and stamina. Faithful and affectionate, though not always obedient.

Origin: Believed to have evolved from white working dogs of the Magyars and have been bred true on the Maremma plains and hills for centuries. It is thought that the first record of a Maremma was 2,000 years ago, when Columbella (about AD 65) refers to a white dog, and Marcus Varro (116-27 BC) provides a standard for a sheepdog not unlike that which exists for the Maremma today.

Grooming: Use a wire brush.

Exercising: Regular rather than extensive, but will adapt to owner's exercise capabilities.

Colouring: All white. A little shading of ivory or pale fawn is permissible.

Desired qualities: Majestic, large, lithe, strongly built and of 'outdoor appearance'.

Drawbacks: None known, except that it has a mind of its own. Any tendency to nervousness or aggression in this breed is highly undesirable.

Mastiff/Bull Mastiff/ Neopolitan Mastiff

Characteristics: Large, powerful dog that makes a brave, loyal and formidable guard. Can be a little tricky with strangers.

Origin: This is a descendant of the fierce dogs that fought in the arenas of ancient Rome. It has existed in Britain since Julius Caesar invaded the British Isles in 55 BC. St Bernard blood has been added. The Bull Mastiff is a separate breed introduced by crossing the Mastiff with the Bulldog, while, the Italian Neopolitan Mastiff has long been used as a guard and tracking dog.

Grooming: Regular brushing.

Exercising: Normal exercising on hard ground.

Colouring: Mastiff: Apricot-fawn, silver-fawn, fawn or dark fawn brindle. Bull Mastiff: Any shade of brindle, fawn or red, colour to be pure and clear. Neopolitan Mastiff: Preferred black, blue, all shades of grey, brown varying from fawn to red.

Desired qualities: A combination of grandeur and courage.

Drawbacks: Not suitable for a child to take for a walk on the lead, or for the inexperienced dog owner. Training is essential.

Miniature Pinscher

Characteristics: Splendid little dog with a hackney gait. It is affectionate, usually healthy, easy to look after and makes a good family pet for town or country.

Origin: A descendant of the German Smooth-Haired Pinscher with perhaps a dash of Greyhound and Dachshund added. Not unlike the English Toy Terrier or, indeed, some of the older type, long-legged, smooth-coated Chihuahuas.

Grooming: Brush daily. A rub down with chamois leather or a silk handkerchief will make the coat shine.

Exercising: Will adapt to its owner's exercise capabilities.

Colouring: Black, blue, chocolate with sharply defined tan markings on cheeks, lips, lower jaw, throat, twin spots above eyes and chest, lower half of forelegs, inside of hindlegs and vent region, lower portion of hocks and feet. Solid red of various shades.

Desired qualities: Well balanced, sturdy, compact and elegant little dog.

Drawbacks: None known.

Newfoundland

Characteristics: A gentle giant that is usually good with children and other animals. The Newfoundland is a fine swimmer, a lovable companion and a good pet for those with sufficient room to accommodate it.

Origin: Originated in the north-east of Canada where it was the traditional life-saving dog. Just as the Border Collie has a natural instinct to round up anything that moves, so the Newfoundland has the overwhelming desire to retrieve anything and anyone from the water and swim with them back to safety. Its ancestors are likely to include Red Indian dogs and Basque sheepdogs.

Grooming: Use a hard brush.

Exercising: Reasonable and regular.

Colouring: Black, brown and Landseer, which is white with black markings only.

Desired qualities: Well balanced. Impresses with strength and great activity. Massive bone.

Drawbacks: None known. But remember that it will cost you far more to feed than would a Chihuahua.

Norwich Terrier/ Norfolk Terrier

Characteristics: Tough, courageous and lovable small terrier that is generally good with children and makes a fine pet. It should be noted that the *Norfolk* Terrier is an identical dog, but whereas the Norwich has erect ears, those of the Norfolk are flat.

Origin: Until 1964 the Norwich and Norfolk Terriers were regarded as one and the same breed. From then on, however, the prick-eared and drop-eared varieties were divided into two separate breeds for show purposes. Likely to have had both the Glen of Imaal and the Irish Terrier in their makeup.

Grooming: The minimum of brushing and trimming.

Exercising: Like most terriers, it is a born hunter and would rather be off chasing rabbits than walking sedately in town. However it is an adaptable little dog.

Colouring: All shades of red, wheaten, black and tan or grizzle. White marks or patches undesirable but permissible.

Desired qualities: Small, low, keen dog, compact and strong with good substance and bone. Honourable scars from fair wear and tear not to be unduly penalised.

Drawbacks: None known.

Nova Scotia Duck Tolling Retriever

Characteristics: Quiet, easily trained dog that is a fine swimmer. It admirably combines the roles of housepet and gundog.

Origin: Originated in the Maritimes and was, until fairly recently, little known outside its native Canada. It has a head like that of the Golden Retriever and is well boned down to strong, webbed feet.

Grooming: Daily brushing.

Exercising: Needs plenty, but will adapt to its owner's exercise capabilities, springing to life when called upon to work.

Colouring: Red or fawn.

Desired qualities: A swimmer with outstanding endurance.

Drawbacks: None known, but the breed is a relative newcomer to Britain and might be difficult to obtain.

Old English Sheepdog

Characteristics: Popular, square-looking sheepdog of great stamina. Has sound temperament and gets on well with children and other pets.

Origin: Usually thought of as a True Brit, and commonly known as the 'Bobtail'. It is, however, likely to have evolved through crossing the Briard with the large Russian Owtscharka which, in turn, is related to the Hungarian sheepdogs. Although the Bobtail has worked as a cattle dog in England, it has long been known simply as a much-loved, shaggy companion, for which a breed club was established as long ago as 1888.

Grooming: Daily brushing. Use a steel comb about once a week. If you intend to exhibit, many hours of preparation are needed. Ask the breeder for advice.

Exercising: Will adapt to owner's exercise capabilities, but don't keep this giant cooped up in a small space.

Colouring: Any shade of grey, grizzle or blue.

Desired qualities: Strong, square-looking dog of great symmetry and overall soundness.

Drawbacks: Despite its good nature, this is a heavy dog and might prove too much for a lightweight to handle. Costs quite a lot to feed.

Otterhound

Characteristics: Appealing and amiable big, strong hound that is a first class swimmer, good with children and has a dense, rough harsh, waterproof coat.

Origin: An ancient breed possibly descended from the Bloodhound and most likely some of the French hounds. When otter hunting was outlawed in the United Kingdom the Otterhound could have been lost had not the Master of the Kendal and District Otter-hounds, in the English Lake District, set up a breed club to ensure the breed's survival. Since that time the Otterhound has developed into a popular show dog and is frequently kept as a pet, though it is not ideally suited for indoor life, and certainly not for that of suburbia.

Grooming: Brushing and combing.

Exercising: Needs plenty.

Colouring: All recognised hound colours permissible: whole coloured, grizzle, sandy, red, wheaten, blue.

Desired qualities: Large, straight-limbed and sound; rough-coated, with majestic head – built for a day's work.

Drawbacks: Even-tempered, but could be destructive if kept indoors.

87

Pekingese

Characteristics: Aloof and glamorous toy dog that is healthy, intelligent and will bestow its favours only after due consideration. Extremely loyal to owners.

Origin: The story is well known of how, following the Boxer rebellion, the summer palace in Peking was invaded and five imperial Pekingese looted by British officers. One of these Pekes, to be christened 'Looty', was presented to Her Majesty, Queen Victoria, lived until 1872, and was painted by the artist, Landseer. Previously, the revered little Pekes were not allowed to be taken outside China. Their imperious manner exists to this day.

Grooming: Use a soft-bristled brush. Requires fairly extensive show preparation. Check with the breeder.

Exercising: Despite its reputation as a lap dog, the Pekingese enjoys nothing better than a country walk.

Colouring: All colourings and markings are permissible and of equal merit, except albino or liver. Parti-colours evenly broken.

Desired qualities: Compact, short-coupled dog, well knit in frame.

Drawbacks: Guard against over-exertion in warm weather. Always travel with a supply of iced water in summer.

Petit Basset Griffon Vendeen

Characteristics: Happy and attractive hound, well balanced, and short-legged. It is a basset reduced in size and proportions, but retaining all the qualities of the breed. A good family companion.

Origin: The Petit Basset Griffon Vendeen, which is now a regular contender in the British show ring, was bred down from the larger Basset Griffon Vendeen, still used in its native France for hunting wild boar.

Grooming: Very little attention needed.

Exercising: Plenty. And remember that, hound-like, it will roam if given the chance.

Colouring: White with any combination of lemon, orange, tri-colour or grizzle markings.

Desired qualities: Strong, active hound, capable of a day's hunting, with a good voice, freely used.

Drawbacks: Only suitable for someone who can provide sufficient space and exercise.

Pharoah Hound

Characteristics: Graceful, noble-looking ancient breed that is affectionate, intelligent and good with children.

Origin: When the Phoenicians settled in Malta and Gozo, they brought these hounds with them. That they have changed little in more than 5,000 years is to the credit of Malta, where the Pharoah Hounds have resided for more than 2,000 years. They were bred for rabbit-hunting and are referred to by the Maltese as the *Keib-Tal-Fenek,* which means 'rabbit dog'. Oft-recorded is the fact that when, in 1935, Dr. George Reisner was working in the Great Pyramid of Cheops at Giza, he discovered an inscription recording the burial of a dog named Abuwtiyuw. The burial was carried out with all the ritual ceremonies accorded to a great man of Egypt, by order of the kings of Upper and Lower Egypt. The dog resembled the Pharoah Hound.

Grooming: Use a hound glove.

Exercising: Needs plenty.

Colouring: Tan or rich tan with certain white markings.

Desired qualities: Medium-sized, of noble bearing with clean-cut lines. Graceful yet powerful. Hunts by sight and scent.

Drawbacks: Not suitable for apartment living. Best in country.

Pointer

Characteristics: Attractive and obedient gundog that is good with children and admirably combines the roles of sportsman's dog and family pet.

Origin: Thought to have originated in Spain, but there is also a school of thought that it is the result of crossing the Greyhound with Bloodhounds and Foxhounds. An authority on the Breed, William Arkwright of Sutton Scarsdale, spent many years researching the pointer breed and, according to his findings, it originated in the East from whence it found its way to Italy and then Spain, where it developed its classic head, and only then did it reach England and South America.

Grooming: Regular brushing.

Exercising: Needs plenty.

Colouring: Usual colours are lemon and white, orange and white, liver and white and black and white. Solid colours and tri-colours are also correct.

Desired qualities: Symmetrical and well built all over, general outline a series of graceful curves.

Drawbacks: None known.

Polish Lowland Dog

Characteristics: Hardy, good-natured guard that resembles an Old English Sheepdog and has only recently appeared on the British show scene. It is easy to train, alert and of good temperament.

Origin: There are two varieties of Polish Sheepdog, the Lowland, which looks like the Bobtail, and a larger dog, more like the Retriever. They were introduced into Poland in the fourth or fifth century, when they were mainly used as herding and watch dogs.

Grooming: Brushing. Also use a steel comb.

Exercising: Needs plenty.

Colouring: All colours acceptable.

Desired qualities: Medium-sized, cobby, strong, muscular.

Drawbacks: None known.

Pomeranian

Characteristics: Delightful and intelligent toy dog that is affectionate, usually good with children and is eminently suitable for apartment living.

Origin: A member of the Spitz family, which takes its name from Pomerania in Germany. The Pom was introduced into a number of European countries in the eighteenth century, when it was a much larger dog than it is today. For a time, Poms were exhibited in classes for those over and under 3.6 kg (8lbs), but challenge certificates for the larger variety were withdrawn as long ago as 1915.

Grooming: Not a breed for those with little time to spend on grooming. Daily attention with a stiff brush is essential. The Pomerania has two coats, a shorter, fluffy undercoat and a long, straight overcoat. Trimming is also required. Ask the breeder for advice if you intend to exhibit.

Exercising: Despite being a lap dog and an obvious choice for the elderly, this is a little dog with plenty of 'get up and go'. I know a Pomeranian which walked miles over the Scottish hills with its owners, and lived to a ripe old age.

Colouring: All colours permissible, provided they are free from black or white shadings.

Desired qualities: Compact, short-coupled dog, well knit in frame.

Drawbacks: Like many little dogs it has a tendency to yap if unchecked.

Poodles (Standard, Miniature and Toy)

Characteristics: Attractive, intelligent and full of fun. All three varieties are devoted and make good show dogs. The smaller varieties in particular are generally long-lived. The Standard Poodle can be taught to retrieve, while all three sizes can be trained for obedience work.

Origin: Started life as a water retriever in Germany, the word *Pudel* being German for 'puddle'. Undoubtedly the breed has common ancestry with the Irish Water Spaniel, the French Barbet and the Hungarian Waterhound. The smaller Poodles were favourites of the French Queen Marie Antoinette, while Prince Rupert of the Rhine took his Poodle into battle with him, when he went to the aid of the unfortunate King Charles I.

Grooming: A wire-pin pneumatic brush and a metal comb are needed. All three varieties are exhibited in the show ring in the lion clip; pet dogs are often kept in a lamb clip. It is best to discuss this matter with the breeder.

Exercising: Standards require plenty of exercise, the smaller varieties will adapt to their owner's capabilities.

Colouring: All solid colours: white, black, silver, blue, brown, apricot, cream.

Desired qualities: Well balanced, elegant looking with very proud carriage.

Drawbacks: None known.

Portuguese Water Dog

Characteristics: An attractive and unusual dog that is loyal and makes an excellent guard. It is a fine swimmer.

Origin: Known around the Iberian Peninsula for many centuries, where its job was to retrieve fish and guard the fishermen's nets. It is also a good rabbit hunter. There is a long-coated variety and a short, curly-coated variety, the latter being rather better known.

Grooming: Daily brushing.

Exercising: Needs plenty. Not a dog for the suburban life.

Colouring: Black, white, various shades of brown, black and white, brown and white.

Desired qualities: This is a tremendously intelligent fisherman's dog.

Drawbacks: Not too keen on strangers.

Pug

Characteristics: Decidedly square and cobby toy
dog that is good with children and makes a
lovable companion.

Origin: Once known as 'Little Turks', Pugs
arrived in France with the Turkish Fleet in 1553
and soon became favourites with the ladies,
including the Empress Josephine, who refused
to be parted from her pet Pug on her wedding
night. It is said that, at one time, Pugs were fed
on so many titbits that they became grotesque
and indeed they still have a sweet tooth.
However, towards the latter part of the last
century, the Pug Dog Club was formed and
efforts made to standardise the breed, which
have been extremely successful.

Grooming: Daily brushing.

Exercising: Enjoy walks on the lead. Should not
be over exerted or taken out in very hot weather.

Colouring: Silver, apricot, fawn or black.

Desired qualities: They should have great charm,
dignity and intelligence, and have a happy and
lively disposition.

Drawbacks: None known. But don't over-feed or
over-exert.

Pyrenean Mountain Dog

Characteristics: Natural guard dog that is lively, intelligent and may, if the owner wishes, be kept in an outside kennel. Loyal and devoted.

Origin: Has guarded flocks for many centuries in the Pyrenees, where it would wear a spiked collar similar to that of the Neopolitan Mastiff. It was also a favourite at the French Court prior to the Revolution. However, it is only in comparatively recent times that it has found international fame as housepet and show dog.

Grooming: Daily brushing.

Exercising: Regular exercise. Sufficient space is of prime importance.

Colouring: Mainly white, with patches of badger, wolf-grey, pale yellow or white.

Desired qualities: Great size, substance and power, looking immensely strong and well balanced.

Drawbacks: Needs careful training. Not the ideal choice for young children.

Rhodesian Ridgeback

Characteristics: Affectionate, intelligent and easily trained, the Ridgeback is a fine guard that is loyal to its family, good with children, but aloof with strangers.

Origin: A descendant of the Hottentot Hunting Dog, to which have been added the best points of a number of other European breeds. Has been used to guard diamond mines in South Africa and will watch over its owners with the same intensity and devotion.

Grooming: Use a hound glove.

Exercising: Needs plenty.

Colouring: Light wheaten to red wheaten. Peculiarity is ridge on back formed by hair growing in opposite direction to the remainder of coat.

Desired qualities: Handsome, strong, muscular and active.

Drawbacks: None known.

Rottweiler

Characteristics: Stalwart dog of above average size. Bold and courageous. Loyal to its owner and a reliable working animal that responds to firm but kindly handling. Not the pet dog for beginners.

Origin: The original butcher's dog from Rottweil in Württemberg. Also known as a hunter of wild boar in the Middle Ages and subsequently as a cattle and draught dog. Unfortunately it has, in recent times, been favoured by those who want to own such a dog for its macho image rather than its fine working abilities.

Grooming: Daily brushing.

Exercising: Benefits from a job of work.

Colouring: Black with clearly defined markings.

Desired qualities: Calm gaze should indicate good humour!

Drawbacks: Not suitable for the inexperienced unless they have time to devote to its training.

Rough Collie

Characteristics: Affectionate, beautiful and easily trained. This is the collie synonymous with the *Lassie* film and television series. It remains a firm favourite.

Origin: Generally thought of as Scottish, but in fact introduced into the United Kingdom from Iceland some 400 years ago. Guarded flocks in Scotland where sheep with black faces and legs were described as 'colleys'. A breed member was kept by Queen Victoria at Balmoral, after she had seen and admired the variety working in the Highlands.

Grooming: Has a thick coat, but daily brushing should suffice.

Exercising: Needs plenty.

Colouring: Sable and white, tri-colour and blue merle.

Desired qualities: A dog of great beauty, standing with impassive dignity, with no part out of proportion to the whole.

Drawbacks: None known.

St. Bernard

Characteristics: Gentle giant that adores children and is easy to train. It does however need a lot of space and is not particularly long-lived. Essential to buy from sound stock.

Origin: Another descendant of the Roman Molossian dogs, but this one is a gentle beast, named after the St. Bernard Hospice in the Swiss Alps where, between 1660 and 1670, it found fame for its prowess in rescuing climbers. In more recent times its popularity has soared because of its association with advertisements for brandy.

Grooming: Daily brushing.

Exercising: Regular, but not necessarily extensive and certainly not too much in youth.

Colouring: Orange, mahogany-brindle, red-brindle, white with patches on body of various named colours.

Desired qualities: Distinctly marked, large-sized mountain rescue dog.

Drawbacks: Short lifespan and tendency to weakness in hindquarters. Need for adequate space – and sufficient funds needed to meet costs of feeding.

Saluki

Characteristics: An ancient and graceful sight hound that is faithful and dignified. Good with children.

Origin: The Saluki takes its name from Saluk in the Yemen. A member of the Greyhound family, it is one of the most ancient breeds and, in common with the Greyhound and Pharaoh Hound, its likeness is depicted on the tombs of the ancient Egyptians. It was at one time known as the Persian Greyhound.

Grooming: Use a hound glove and/or soft brush. Gently comb ears and tail fringes.

Exercising: Capable of immense speed and not the dog to keep in confined quarters.

Colouring: White, cream, fawn, golden red, grizzle, silver grizzle, deer grizzle, tri-colour (white, black and tan and variations of these colours, i.e. black fringed fawn, black fringed red), not brindle.

Desired qualities: Faithful, with far-seeing eyes. General impression of grace and symmetry. Great speed and endurance, coupled with its strength and activity.

Drawbacks: None known. But remember that it has strong hunting instincts.

Samoyed

Characteristics: Beautiful, white Spitz variety that, unlike most of its fellows, makes a good pet and show dog, and often works well in obedience. Hardy and devoted.

Origin: The Samoyed comes from Siberia, its name deriving from the tribe of Samoyedes. It is a sled dog in its homeland and breed members accompanied the explorer, Nansen, on his trip to the North Pole.

Grooming: Brushing, combing and towelling.

Exercising: Needs plenty and, if possible, a job of work to do.

Colouring: Pure white, white and biscuit, cream, outer coat silver-tipped.

Desired qualities: The 'Sammy' should have a smiling expression.

Drawbacks: None except that in common with other long-haired, light-coated breeds, it does 'shed'.

Schnauzer (Giant, Standard and Miniature)

Characteristics: There are three Schnauzers, Giant, Standard and Miniature, the last being the most popular type in Britain. However, they all share the qualities of good humour and affection. Good with children, easy to train and splendid at obedience work.

Origin: The Miniature Schnauzer is probably the result of a crossing between the larger standard Schnauzer and the Affenpinscher, perhaps with a dash of Fox Terrier. Schnauzers were evolved from German sheepdogs and the Giant through the interbreeding with smaller Schnauzer varieties. A statue exists in Stuttgart, dated 1620, showing a watchman with a dog similar to the Schnauzer of today. The breed originated in Bavaria and Württemberg and when its original job of cattle-driving ceased it found its way into the hearts of the public as a good-natured pet.

Grooming: Daily brush. Twice yearly trim.

Exercising: Enjoys a game. Will adapt to owner's capabilities.

Colouring: Pure black or pepper and salt.

Desired qualities: A dog that is sturdily built, robust, sinewy and nearly square. Primarily a companion dog.

Drawbacks: None known.

Scottish Terrier

Characteristics: Home-loving, fun-loving terrier that is utterly loyal to its owners but not interested in strangers. It is a good watch dog.

Origin: A true Scot, formerly known as the Aberdeen Terrier, the 'Scottie' has been around for centuries, but did not achieve its own Kennel Club breed standard until 1892, when the breed club was formed.

Grooming: Brushing, combing and seasonal trimming.

Exercising: Loves a walk – and a game. Just the dog to play ball games with.

Colouring: Black, wheaten or brindle of any shade.

Desired Qualities: Thick set, of suitable size to go to ground. Bold, but never aggressive.

Drawbacks: Could be jealous if, for instance, a child was introduced into the household.

Shar-Pei

Characteristics: Most unusual dog, of Chinese origin, with loose skin and a frowning expression. It is usually good-tempered, highly intelligent – and ownership makes a fine talking point.

Origin: The Shar-Pei (Chinese Fighting Dog) was bred to hunt wild boar and also as a herder. It appears to have been in existence since the Hans Dynasty (206 BC to AD 220). Although used as a fighting dog for many centuries – its loose skin making it difficult for an adversary to catch hold – aggression is not in its nature and it is believed that it was probably provoked. It is also said that it may have escaped the cooking pot, the fate of other Chinese breeds, because its flesh was not very tasty.

Grooming: Regular brushing.

Exercising: Enjoys plenty.

Colouring: Solid colours – black, red, light or dark shades of fawn and cream.

Desired Qualities: Alert, active, compact, short-coupled and squarely built.

Drawbacks: Few, now that the breed has become established in Britain.

Shetland Sheepdog

Characteristics: Beautiful and intelligent 'Lassie' in miniature. Devoted to owners and does well in obedience.

Origin: Evolved in the Shetland Isles of Scotland where it developed a thick coat as protection against the elements. It has bred true for some 150 years.

Grooming: Brush and comb. Use stiff, bristled brush.

Exercising: Will adapt to owner's exercise capabilities. Enjoys obedience work.

Colouring: Sables, tri-colours, blue merles. Black and white and black and tan are also recognised colours.

Desired Qualities: Small, long haired working dog of great beauty.

Drawbacks: None known. But remember that this little sheepdog is a housepet, not a kennel dog.

Shiba Inu

Characteristics: A comparative newcomer to Britain that is proving popular as a pet, show dog, companion and guard.

Origin: The Shiba is the smallest of the Japanese Spitz breeds, and together with the Japanese Akita, and another lesser-known spitz, the Ainou, it is one of the main breeds within the group. Originating in central Japan it was not registered until 1928, although it is thought to have been in existence for very many years, fulfilling the role of companion, guard and hunter of birds and small game.

Grooming: Regular brushing.

Exercising: Likes plenty.

Colouring: Red, salt and pepper, black, black and tan or white.

Desired Qualities: Short, broad skull with pointed face and dark brown eyes. Small, triangular, pricked ears.

Drawbacks: None known. Friendly temperament.

Shih Tzu (Chrysanthemum Dog)

Characteristics: The Shih Tzu is affectionate, hardy and intelligent, revels in attention and usually gets on well with children, and other pets.

Origin: The Lhasa Apso was highly prized by the Dalai Lama of Tibet, who gave choice specimens to emperors of China. Most likely the Chinese crossed the Apso with the Pekingese to produce the Shih Tzu. Export from China was forbidden until the death of Empress Tzu-hsi in 1908 when a few Shih Tzus, like the Pekingese, were smuggled out of China.

Grooming: Not a breed for those without time on their hands. Daily brushing with a brush of pure bristles is essential. Tangles must be combed out. The topknot is usually tied back with a bow.

Exercising: Enjoy regular exercise, whether in the park or a farm yard.

Colouring: All colours allowed. A white blaze on the forehead and a white-tipped tail are highly prized.

Desired Qualities: A very active and alert little dog with an arrogant expression.

Drawbacks: Only the amount of grooming required.

Siberian Husky

Characteristics: A Spitz variety that is hardy, friendly and outgoing. Needs lots of exercise and is a willing worker.

Origin: Bred by the nomadic Ckukchi tribes of north-east Asia with the sole purpose of producing a dog that would ideally combine the roles of working sled dog, friend and hunter. It has, however, proved itself in more recent times as search and rescue dog, sled-racing dog, and show dog.

Grooming: Regular brushing.

Exercising: Needs plenty. Not suited to suburban living.

Colouring: All colours and markings including white allowed.

Desired Qualities: Medium-sized working sled dog, quick and light on feet.

Drawbacks: This dog, with its great powers of speed and endurance, is not suitable for confinement in a small area.

Skye Terrier

Characteristics: Long, low, profusely coated terrier from the Scottish islands. It is a one-man dog, though never vicious, and is elegant and dignified.

Origin: Famed throughout the world, mainly because of the legend of 'Greyfriars Bobby' and the commemorative statue at Greyfriars Churchyard in Edinburgh. You can even buy silver teaspoons – indeed I have one – commemorating the faithful Bobby. The Skye evolved from small earth dogs kept in Scotland to hunt foxes and other vermin, and appears to have been bred true for many hundreds of years.

Grooming: Daily brushing and combing. Use a wide-toothed comb. Ask the breeder for advice if you intend to show.

Exercising: Enjoys a romp, despite that glamorous coat.

Colouring: Black, dark or light grey, fawn or cream, all with black points.

Desired Qualities: Long and low, back level. Rib-cage oval, deep and long. Short loin. Sides appear flattish due to straight-falling coat.

Drawbacks: The amount of grooming necessary and its distrust of strangers.

Soft-Coated Wheaten Terrier

Characteristics: Hardy, rarely seen terrier that is full of fun and makes a gentle and devoted pet.

Origin: Traces back at least 200 years in Ireland, where there was hardly a homestead without one. Reckoned to be the oldest Irish terrier, it could well have had a hand in producing those other Irish terriers, the Kerry Blue and the Irish.

Grooming: Needs daily combing.

Exercising: A natural rabbit and vermin hunter, it will also adapt to its owner's exercise capabilities, but don't keep this lover of fresh air confined.

Colouring: A good, clear wheaten that is the shade of ripening corn.

Desired Qualities: A natural terrier with strong sporting instincts, hardy and of strong constitution.

Drawbacks: None known. But remember that, despite its love of the outdoors, it is essentially a housedog.

Staffordshire Bull Terrier

Characteristics: Attractive, friendly bull terrier that generally adores children and its human family, but can be something of a menace with other dogs.

Origin: Once a fighting dog and still not averse to taking on its fellows, the lovable Staffie is the result of crossing a Bulldog with a terrier, probably the old Black and Tan. Today it has many devotees and is a popular show dog.

Grooming: Daily brushing.

Exercising: Needs a good garden to romp in and regular walks on the lead.

Colouring: Red, fawn, white, black or blue or any of these colours with white.

Desired Qualities: Smooth-coated, well balanced, of great strength for his size. Muscular, active and agile.

Drawbacks: Tend to have minds of their own and many, *though not all,* enjoy a scrap.

NB The Staffordshire Bull Terrier should not be confused with the American Staffordshire Terrier (or Pit Bull) which has been developed along quite different lines.

Sussex Spaniel

Characteristics: Seldom seen, massive and strongly built spaniel that moves with a decided roll. It is loyal, intelligent, and has an excellent nose.

Origin: A 'True Brit', the Sussex Spaniel takes its name from its county of origin, where it was developed by a Mr. Fuller in 1798. The variety was then somewhat larger than it is today. Clumber blood was added between the wars to ensure the continuance of the breed, but this appears only to have improved matters.

Grooming: Brushing and combing. Take care of ears (see Cocker Spaniel).

Exercising: Best suited to country life.

Colouring: Rich, golden liver and hair shading to golden at tips; gold predominating.

Desired Qualities: Massive, strongly built, active, energetic dog. Natural working ability.

Drawbacks: Tends to disregard all but its master, if that is a drawback.

Swedish Vallhund

Characteristics: Charming Swedish breed, not unlike the Welsh Corgi. It is active, affectionate, and also, like the Corgi, it is a good cattle dog, friendly, and eager to please.

Origin: The development of the Swedish Vallhund, (or Vastgotaspets) is generally credited to the Swedish breeder, Bjorn von Rosen. It would seem that the British Corgi did play a part in its makeup, and this probably occurred as the result of Vikings taking British dogs to Sweden – or vice versa. In recent times the Vallhund has certainly made its mark on the British show scene.

Grooming: Daily brushing.

Exercising: Does best in the country but will adapt to its owner's exercise capabilities.

Colouring: Steel grey, greyish-brown, greyish-yellow, reddish-yellow, reddish-brown with darker guard hairs on specific places.

Desired Qualities: Small, powerful, sturdily built working dog, with fairly long body.

Drawbacks: None known. May share the Corgi's reputation as an occasional nipper!

Tibetan Spaniel

Characteristics: Happy, highly assertive and
   intelligent little dog, not unlike a Pekingese. It
   is still fairly unusual, although a popular
   contender in the show ring. It is good with
   children, suitable for town or country, and is an
   excellent choice of household pet.

Origin: First found in a Tibetan monastery,
   where its job was to turn the prayer wheel. It is
   related to both the Lhasa Apso and the Tibetan
   Terrier, but resembles a Pekingese with a touch
   of toy spaniel.

Grooming: Daily brushing.

Exercising: Will adapt to its owner's exercise
   capabilities.

Colouring: All colours and mixtures of colours
   permissible.

Desired Qualities: Small, active and alert. Well
   balanced in general outline; slightly longer in
   body than height at withers.

Drawbacks: None known. Good pet choice.

Weimaraner

Characteristics: Unusual and attractive gundog that excels in agility and obedience, is a fine gundog and combines these abilities with that of an affectionate household pet. It does best if kept indoors as a family member rather than in an outside kennel.

Origin: Developed as a gundog in Weimar Germany during the latter part of the eighteenth century. The Old St. Hubert Hound, the Pointer and the Bloodhound are each said to have had a hand in its makeup. Since appearing on the British show scene in the 1950s, it has also made its mark as a Police dog.

Grooming: Daily brushing.

Exercising: Needs plenty.

Colouring: Preferably silver grey, with shades of mouse or roe grey permissible. It is nicknamed 'the silver ghost'.

Desired Qualities: Medium-sized, grey with light eyes. Presents a picture of power, stamina and balance.

Drawbacks: None known. But it is unfair to keep this hunting dog in a confined space.

Welsh Corgi (Cardigan and Pembroke)

Characteristics: Attractive and devoted small guards that are outgoing and friendly; also good with children. It is said that the Cardigan has a quieter temperament than the Pembroke, and perhaps does not nip the heels of visitors, a habit inherited from the breed's cattle-herding days.

Origin: Both types worked in South Wales for many centuries since, indeed, the Domesday Book was compiled at the request of William the Conqueror in the eleventh century. As a cattle-herder, the Corgi would control the movement of cattle by nipping at their ankles. The Pembroke has a short tail while that of the Cardigan is moderately long, like a fox's brush. The Cardigan was granted separate classification in 1934.

Grooming: Daily brushing.

Exercising: Will generally adapt to its owner's exercise capabilities. But don't under-exert as the breed has a tendency to put on weight.

Colouring: Cardigan: Any colour, with or without white markings, but white should not predominate. Pembroke: Self-colours in red, sable, fawn, black and tan with or without white markings on legs, brisket and neck.

Desired Qualities: Cardigan: Sturdy, tough, mobile, capable of endurance. Pembroke: Long set, strong, sturdily built.

Drawbacks: Lots of competition in the show ring.

118

Welsh Springer Spaniel

Characteristics: Attractive and tireless working spaniel that is sometimes mistaken for the English Springer. It is loyal, affectionate, and admirably combines the roles of family pet and gundog.

Origin: Similar to the Brittany, formerly known as the Brittany Spaniel. However, a dog similar to the Welsh is mentioned in the earliest records of the Laws of Wales, circa 1300, so it has certainly been around for a long time.

Grooming: Regular brushing and combing. Pay attention to ears (see Cocker Spaniel).

Exercising: Best suited to country life.

Colouring: Rich red and white only.

Desired Qualities: Symmetrical, compact, not leggy. Obviously built for endurance and hard work.

Drawbacks: None known. Best suited to an active life though.

West Highland White Terrier

Characteristics: Smart, game and hardy small terrier that is good with children, gets on well with other pets and makes an ideal choice of family pet for town or country.

Origin: The popular 'Westie' was given its breed standard in 1905, when other Scottish terriers such as the Cairn and Skye went their separate ways, previously having been grouped together as Small Highland Working Terriers. However, as early as the late 1800s, there was a white Scottish terrier developed by a Colonel Malcolm of Poltalloch, which could well have been an ancestor of the Westie. This strain was known as the Portalloch Terrier. Another name bestowed on the white terriers was Roseneath.

Grooming: Brushing and combing. But if you want to exhibit this dog you have quite a task ahead and it would be as well to talk with the breeder about matters such as chalking and hand-stripping.

Exercising: The Westie is a lively character, but will generally adapt to its owner's exercise capabilities.

Colouring: White only.

Desired Qualities: Strongly built, deep in chest and back ribs, level back and powerful quarters on muscular legs.

Drawbacks: None known.

Whippet

Characteristics: Elegant and gentle dog that is clean, affectionate, and ideally combines the roles of housepet and watchdog with that of track racer, if required. Also a popular show dog.

Origin: The Whippet is obviously closely allied to the Greyhound. It was exhibited at Crufts Dog Show as long ago as 1897 but its origin remains a mystery. It is believed that the Greyhound may have been crossed with a terrier or, indeed, a Pharaoh Hound, which would seem more likely.

Grooming: Brushing.

Exercising: Will adapt to most living conditions, but must have plenty of exercise.

Colouring: Any colour or mixture of colours.

Desired Qualities: Balanced combination of muscular power and strength with elegance and grace of outline.

Drawbacks: None known. Highly adaptable in domestic and sporting surroundings.

Yorkshire Terrier

Characteristics: Lovable, fearless small terrier that is convinced it is enormous. Good watchdog, that will adapt to town or country living. Makes a devoted companion.

Origin: A comparatively modern breed, having been developed just over a hundred years ago by crossing the old Black and Tan Terrier with the Skye Terrier and perhaps a dash of Maltese and/or Dandie Dinmont. It was bred to tackle rats, and retains its sporting instincts.

Grooming: Brushing and combing. If it is the owner's intention to exhibit, you have a tough task ahead and your 'Yorkie' will need to have its hair elaborately set with paper curlers. Discuss requirements fully with breeder.

Exercising: The Yorkie will adapt to its owner's exercise capabilities. It is unlikely to tire.

Colouring: Dark steel blue (not silver blue). Hair on chest rich, bright tan.

Desired Qualities: Alert, intelligent toy terrier.

Drawbacks: Like many small dogs it may yap, if it can get away with it. Also time must be spent on show preparation.

Choosing a Dog

The average lifespan of the dog is about twelve years. Toy breeds like the Yorkshire Terrier, Miniature Poodle and others often achieve a few years more. On the other hand, the Great Dane and the Bulldog are lucky if they reach eight or nine years. But whichever breed you choose, it is going to be with you a long time – hence the importance of choosing a breed not just because you like the look of it. But because it meets your requirements in terms of character, size, temperament and, if necessary, working ability. Your lifestyle must be taken into consideration. A Border Collie is not the dog for apartment living any more than a French Bulldog should be expected to work sheep. The cost of feeding, your own fitness and exercise capabilities, and the time you have available for grooming and training must be borne in mind.

Working breeds, the category under which most sheepdogs and guarding varieties fall, are best suited to a country environment or, at any rate, a home where they will be given a job of work to do (preferably the task for which they were bred), or allowed to compete in agility or obedience at a hobbyists club.

Terriers are extremely lively dogs bred predominantly to hunt small mammals, and while they are lovable and make good pets, they are not ideally suited to the elderly and sedate.

Hounds make loving companions but, true to their origin, most have the urge to wander; while gundogs are generally gentle and loving and will fulfil the dual roles of sporting dog and family pet.

Most of the breeds in the Non-Sporting Group (in Britain this is often called Utility) make the best housepets because, like those in the toy category, they have been bred for no other purpose than that of companion.

If you are looking for a watchdog, do bear in mind that a nervous burglar is just as likely to be put off by the persistent yapping of a small dog behind a closed door as he would be by the growl of a Mastiff.

Feeding, Caring and Training

Feeding

The responsible breeder will give puppy buyers a diet sheet. Basically, however, from the time the pup is collected, probably at eight to twelve weeks of age, it is going to need four meals a day. These should be given in the morning, at midday, in the afternoon and at bed-time. Once the pet is a year old it will need only one meal a day.

Ideally the breakfast and bed-time feeds should consist of a branded baby food, such as Complan, a teaspoon or so of which, mixed with milk and a little sugar, should provide the pup with an appetising milky porridge.

The midday and late afternoon feeds should comprise a saucerful of lean, minced beef which has been lightly cooked and to which a teaspoonful of Marmite or other flavouring may be added to taste. (Some breeders advocate feeding raw meat – this is purely a matter of individual preference.) The meat meals should be supplemented with puppemeal or biscuit in the proportion of three parts meat and two parts biscuit. Meat and milk should never be given at the same time. Make sure that your pet always has access to water.

Nowadays it is possible to obtain excellent canned puppy food and while I personally prefer to start a puppy off with minced beef, there is no reason why a canned product should not be used if the owner wishes. In addition to the feeds mentioned, some of the larger breeds also benefit from an egg whisked in milk at bed-time.

When your pup reaches four months of age, you can omit the bed-time feed and at six months discontinue breakfast. It is up to you whether you wish to divide the pet's remaining meal into two portions, given at different times of the day, once it has become an adult. Toy breeds often do fare better given two small meals, rather than one large one.

Knowing how much food to give the adult dog should be a simple matter. It is, after all, laid down on the label of almost every can of dog food. It must be realised, however, that dogs – like people – are individuals and while one may put on weight easily, another may remain sylph-like despite a hearty appetite.

Obviously the dog in regular work is likely to need more generous rations than its contemporary which does little but sit at the fireside. Nevertheless, if its weight differs considerably from that laid down in its breed standard, it would be advisable to discuss the problem with a veterinarian.

The food requirements of breeds can be categorised into those for toy, small, medium and large dogs. Given that the standard tin of dog food contains about 13½ ozs (380g), a toy breed needs ¼ – ½ can per day; a small dog, like a West Highland White Terrier needs ½ can; a French Bulldog about ¾ can; and a dog of Labrador or German Shepherd Dog size 1½ cans or more.

Caring

Caring for your dog means ensuring that it has a comfortable bed placed in a warm, draught-free position, that it has adequate exercise and toys to play with, that it is groomed, wormed, and taken to the veterinarian for regular check-ups and boosters as well as for its initial inoculations.

You should not, under any circumstances, walk your puppy on the street until it has had its inoculations against the killer diseases distemper, canine viral hepatitis, leptospirosis, parvo-virus and kennel cough. This usually entails a single jab embracing all these diseases at around twelve weeks old, with another two or three weeks later.

If you have decided to have a bitch rather than a dog, and do not intend to breed from her, it would be sensible to discuss with the veterinarian the possibility of having her spayed, so that she will not have twice-yearly seasons. It is possible, although not inexpensive, for the bitch to have inoculations to put off seasons and you should discuss the various alternatives with your vet.

Do remember that should you wish to go away on holiday, or even on business for a few days, arrangements will have to be made for your pet. Good boarding kennels get booked up well ahead, so it is sensible to make a reservation at the same time as arranging your own accommodation. You will be expected to show the proprietor your dog's up to date inoculation record card and to provide evidence of protection against kennel cough, if this was not included in the inoculation given.

There are hotels that accept canine guests but it is vital to check out the position with the management before turning up with your pet.

Please note that all dogs entering the United Kingdom from overseas are subject to quarantine for a six-month period in kennels approved by the Ministry of Agriculture, Fisheries and Food. Buyers wishing to take dogs outside the United Kingdom should check with the relevant embassy regarding health regulations.

Training

Training is part of caring; not just house and lead training but teaching your pet to be a good citizen that does not foul the streets, jump up at visitors or bark other than to give a brief warning.

Nowadays almost every town and village has a dog

training club. Owners attend club meetings with their dog on one or two evenings a week so that the dog may learn basic obedience and, importantly, to socialise with other dogs – and humans.

Addresses of dog training clubs may be obtained from the Kennel Club, your veterinarian, the local library or your nearest pet shop.

Showing Dogs

Showing dogs means getting up in the small hours of the morning to drive to championship shows at the other end of the country, often returning tired and disappointed late at night. But there is nothing to compare with the thrill of a win, and the comradeship of a hobby that enables one to meet friends from far afield at the various venues.

Many people imagine that, if a dog has a Certificate of Pedigree, it is a natural candidate for the show ring. This is not the case. A Certificate of Pedigree proves that the dog is pure-bred. It records its parentage for three, or perhaps five generations, and while the dog may be an attractive, healthy specimen of its breed, this does not necessarily mean that it is up to show standard.

Each variety has a standard of perfection, the 'breed standard', laid down by the Kennel Club. It is the exhibit that most exactly meets that standard which is awarded a prize card, or rosette, in the show ring.

Many pure-bred dogs are unsuitable for showing for any number of reasons. They may be too big or too small, incorrectly coloured or may not have an even bite.

If you ask a breeder to sell you a dog with a Certificate of Pedigree (in other words, a dog of a known variety) this does not mean that they have to sell you a show dog. In any case, there is never any guarantee that a pup is destined to be a champion. If, however, you have the desire to exhibit, do make your wishes plain to the breeder and they will do their best to pick out a likely prospect for you.

Almost without exception, every breed has its own breed club, which holds shows for the variety. These prove an excellent training ground for novice exhibitors, and enables them to pick up many tips from more seasoned campaigners. It is also likely that in your town or village there will be a Ringcraft class which – unlike the dog training class, which teaches obedience – concentrates on preparing dog and owner for the show ring. Addresses of these classes can be obtained from the Kennel Club, your veterinarian, the local library or your nearest pet shop. Dog shows are advertised in the weekly canine press (see useful addresses).

Short Glossary of Terms

Belton   A colour designation. An intermingling of coloured and white hairs.

Blaze   A white stripe running up the centre of the face, usually between the eyes.

Blenheim   Ground pearl white, with well distributed chestnut red patches.

Blue   Usually dark steely blue.

Cobby   Short-bodied, compact

Hackney-gait
   The high lifting of the front feet, like that of a Hackney horse.

Hand-stripping
   Stripping out the coat by hand.

Harlequin   Patched or pied coloration, usually black and white.

Hocks   The tarsus or collection of bones of the hind leg forming the joint between the second thigh and the metatarsus, the dog's true heel.

Isabella   Fawn or light brown.

Mask   Dark shading on the foreface.

Merle   Flecked eye, brown and blue with black iris.

Pencilling   Black lines on the toes.

Pinto   Black and white, or brown and white, like Pinto horse.

Self-colours
   Whole colours.

Short-coupled
   With very short coupling.

Vent   The anal opening.

Withers   The highest point of the body immediately behind the neck.

Useful Addresses

United Kingdom

The Agility Club, The Spinney, Aubrey Lane, Redbourn, Herts AL3 7AN.

Animal Health Trust, PO Box 5, Newmarket, Suffolk CB8 7DW.

Animal Welfare Trust, Tylers Way, Watford Bypass, Watford, Herts.

Assistance Dogs for the Disabled, 23 Slipper Road, Emsworth, Hants PO10 8BS.

Battersea Dogs' Home, 4 Battersea Park Road, London SW8 4AA.

Birmingham Dogs' Home, New Bartholomew Street, Birmingham B5 5QS.

The Blue Cross, Shilton Road, Burford, Oxon OX8 4PF.

British Association for German Shepherd Dogs, 64 Kings Road, Erdington, Birmingham B23 7JS.

British Field Sports Society, 59 Kennington Road, London SE1 7PZ.

British Homoeopathic Association, 27a Devonshire Street, London W1N 1RJ.

British Small Animals Veterinary Association, 7 Mansfield Street, London W1M 0AT.

British Veterinary Association, 7 Mansfield Street, London W1M 0AT.

Canine Studies Institute, London Road, Bracknell, Berks RG12 4HR.

Dogs Breeders' Insurance, reference 27825 (insurance for veterinary fees), 9 St. Stephens Road, Bournemouth BH2 6LG.

Guide Dogs for the Blind Association, Alexandra

House, Park Street, Windsor, Berks SL4 1JR.

Hearing Dogs for the Deaf, The Training Centre, London Road (A40) Lewknor, Oxford OX9 5RY.

International Sheep Dog Society, 64 Loyes Street, Bedford MK40 1EZ.

The Kennel Club (See separate entry).

National Canine Defence League, 1 Pratt Mews, London NW1 0AD.

People's Dispensary for Sick Animals, PDSA House, South Street, Dorking, Surrey.

PRO Dogs, Rocky Bank, New Road, Ditton, Maidstone, Kent ME20 6AD.

Royal Society for the Prevention of Cruelty to Animals (RSPCA), Causeway, Horsham, West Sussex RH12 1HG.

Society for Companion Animal Studies, (Mrs. Anne Docherty, Director), The Mews Cottage, 7 Botanic Crescent Lane, Glasgow G20 8AA.

Overseas

American Animal Hospital Association, 3612 East Jefferson, South Bend, Indiana 46615.

American Humane Association (incorporating **The Hearing Dog Association)**, 5351 Roslyn, Denver, Colorado 80201.

American Society for the Prevention of Cruelty to Animals, 441 East 92nd Street, New York, New York 10028.

Animal Welfare Institute, PO Box 3650, Washington DC 20007.

Guide Dogs for the Blind, PO Box 1200 San Rafael, California 94902.

Owner Handler Association of America, 583 Knoll Court, Seaford, New York 11783.

Rare Breeds Association, 31 Byram Bay Road, Hopatcong, New Jersey 07843.

The Kennel Club

The Kennel Club will provide addresses for breeders of any dog. It should be noted that only a very brief summary of the Kennel Club's official breed standard has been mentioned under 'Desired Qualities' in the Almanac, and that prospective buyers wishing to study the finer points of a breed's standard should discuss this matter with the relevant breed club representative.

If you wish to obtain an older, pure-bred dog, or one that is in need of re-homing, please apply to the Kennel Club for a copy of their Breed Rescue List.

1-4 Clarges Street, Piccadilly, London W1Y 8AB.

Kennel Clubs overseas can be contacted at the following addresses:

Australia, National Kennel Council, Royal Show Grounds, Ascot Vale, Victoria.

Belgium, Societé Royale Saint-Hubert, Avenue de l'Armée 25, B-1040, Brussels.

Bermuda, Bermuda Kennel Club Inc. PO Box 1455, Hamilton 5.

Brazil, Brazil Kennel Club, Caixa Postal, 1468, Rio de Janeiro.

Canada, Canadian Kennel Cub, 2150 Bloor Street West, Toronto M6S 1M8, Ontario.

Caribbean, Caribbean Kennel Club, PO Box 737, Port of Spain, Trinidad.

Chile, Kennel Club de Chile, Casilla 1704, Valparaiso.

Columbia, Club Canino Colombiano, Calle 70, No. 4-60, 3er Piso, Bogota D.E. Columbia.

Denmark, Dansk Kennelklub Parkvj 1, Jersie Strand, 2680 Solrad Strand.

East Africa, East Africa Kennel Club, PO Box 14223, St. Andrews Church, Nyerere Road, Nairobi, Kenya.

Finland, Suomen Kennellitto-Finska Kennelklubben, Bulevardi 14A, Helsinki.

France, Societé Centrale Canine, 215 Rue St. Denis, 75083 Paris.

Germany, Verband Für das Deutsche Hundewesen (VDH) Postlach 1390, 46 Dortmund.

Guernsey, Guernsey Kennel Club, Myrtle Grove, St. Jacques, Guernsey, CI.

Holland, Raad van Beheer op Kynologisch Gebied in Nederland, Emmalaan 16, Amsterdam Z.

Hong Kong, Hong Kong Kennel Club, 3rd Floor, 28B Stanley Street, Hong Kong.

India, Kennel Club of India, 17 Mukathal Street, Purasawaltam, Madras 600 007.

Ireland, Irish Kennel Club, 23 Earlsfort Terrace, Dublin 2.

Italy, Ente Nazionale Della Cinofilia Italiana, Viale Premuda 21, Milan.

Jamaica, Jamaican Kennel Cub, 8 Orchard Street, Kingston 5, Jamaica.

Jersey, Jersey Dog Club, Coburg House, Rue-es-Picots, Trinity, Jersey, CI.

Malaysia, Malaysian Kennel Association, No. 8. Jalan Tun Mohd Faud Dua, Taman Tun, Dr Ismail, Kuala Lumpur.

Malta, Main Kennel Club, c/o Msida Youth Centre, 15 Rue d'Argens, Str Msida, Malta, GC.

Monaco, Societé Canine de Monaco, Palais des Congres, Avenue d'Ostende, Monte Carlo.

Nepal, Nepal Kennel Club, PO Box 653, Kathmandu, Nepal.

New Zealand, New Zealand Kennel Club, Private Bag, Porirua, New Zealand.

Norway, Norsk Kennelklub, Teglverksgt 8, Rodelökka, Postboks 6598, Oslo 5.

Pakistan, The Kennel Club of Pakistan, 17a Khayaban-i-iqbal, Shalimar 7, Islamabad.

Portugal, Cluba Portugese de Canicultura, Praca D Joao da Camara 4–3 Lisbon 2.

Singapore, The Singapore Kennel Club, 170 Upper

Bukit Timah Road, 12.02 Singapore 2158.

Scotland, The Scottish Kennel Club, 3 Brunswick Place, Edinburgh.

South Africa, Kennel Union of Southern Africa, 6th Floor, Bree Castle, 68 Bree Street, Cape Town 8001, South Africa, PO Box 11280.

Spain, Real Sociedad Central de Formento de las Razas en Espana, Los Madrazo 20, Madrid 14.

Sweden, Svenska Kennelklubben, Norrbyvagan 30, Box 11043, 161 11 Bromma.

Switzerland, Schweizerische Kynologische Gesellschaft, Falkenplatz 11, 3012, Bern.

United States of America, American Kennel Club, 51 Madison Avenue, New York NY 10010; also: The United Kennel Club Inc., 100 East Kilgore Road, Kalamazoo MI 49001-5598.

Uruguay, Kennel Club Uruguayo, Avda Uruguay 864, Montevideo.

Zambia, Kennel Association of Zambia, PO Box 30662, Lusaka.

Publications

Periodicals

Agility Voice, 100 Bedford Road, Barton Le Clay, Beds MK45 4LR.

Dog World, 9 Tufton Street, Ashford, Kent TN23 1QN.

The Kennel Gazette, 1-4 Clarges Street, Piccadilly, London W1Y 8AB.

Obedience Competitor, Long Meadows, Mooredges, Thorne, Doncaster, Yorks DN8 5RY.

Our Dogs, 5 Oxford Road, Station Approach, Manchester M60 1SX.

PetDogs Magazine, Shires Mace Ltd., PO Box 5163, Huddersfield HD4 7YZ.

Overseas Publications

Dog World, Maclean Hunter Publishing Corporation, 29 North Wacker Drive, Chicago Il.

El Mundo del Perro, C/San Romualdo 26, Madrid, Spain.

Onze Hond, CM-Zuidgroep, Abonnementen Service, Postbus 245, 5680, AE BEST Netherlands.

Pure-Bred Dogs/American Kennel Gazette, 51 Madison Avenue, New York, NY 10010.

Bibliography

A Dog of Your Own, Joan Palmer (Salamander Books).

Dog Facts, Joan Palmer (Stanley Paul).

The International Encyclopaedia of Dogs, Ed. Stanley Dangerfield and Elsworth Howell (Mermaid Books).

A Standard Guide to Pure-Bred Dogs, Harry Glover (Macmillan).

The Dog, Fernand Mery (Cassell).

The Encyclopaedia of Dogs, Fiorenzo Fiorone (Hart-Davis, MacGibbon).

Canine Groups

Breeds recognised in the United Kingdom are listed below in the Groups to which they are allocated.

Gundog Group

Brittany
English Setter
German Shorthaired Pointer
German Wirehaired Pointer
Gordon Setter
Hungarian Vizla
Irish Red and White Setter
Irish Setter
Italian Spinone
Large Munsterlander
Pointer
Retriever (Chesapeake Bay)
Retriever (Curly-Coated)
Retriever (Flat-Coated)
Retriever (Golden)
Retriever (Labrador)
Spaniels (American Cocker)
Spaniel (Clumber)
Spaniel (Cocker)
Spaniel (English Springer)
Spaniel (Field)
Spaniel (Irish Water)
Spaniel (Sussex)
Spaniel (Welsh Springer)
Weimaraner

Toy Group

Affenpinscher
Australian Silky Terrier
Bichon Frise
Cavalier King Charles Spaniel
Chihuahua (Long-Coated)
Chihuahua (Smooth-Coated)
Chinese Crested Dog
English Toy Terrier (Black and Tan)
Griffon Bruxellois
Italian Greyhound
Japanese ChinKing CHarles Spaniel
Lowchen (Little Lion Dog)

Maltese
Miniature Pinshcer
Papillon
Pekingese
Pomerania
Pug
Yorkshire Terrier

Utility Group

Boston Terrier
Bulldog
Canaan Dog
Chow Chow
Dalmatian
French Bulldog
German Spitz (Klein)
German Spitz (Mittel)
Japanese Akita
Japanese Shiba Inus
Japanese Spitz
Keeshond
Leonberger
Lhasa Apso
Miniature Schnauzer
Poodle (Miniature)
Poodle (Standard)
Poodle (Toy)
Schipperke
Schnauzer
Shar-Pei
Shih Tzu
Tibetan Spaniel
Tibetan Terrier

Terrier Group

Airedale Terrier
Australian Terrier
Bedlington Terrier
Border Terrier
Bull Terrier
Bull Terrier (Miniature)
Cairn Terrier
Dandie Dinmont Terrier
Fox Terricr (Smooth)
Fox Terrier (Wire)
Glen of Imaal Terrier
Irish Terrier
Kerry Blue Terrier

Lakeland Terrier
Manchester Terrier
Norfolk Terrier
Norwich Terrier
Parson Jack Russell Terrier
Skye Terrier
Soft-Coated Wheaten Terrier
Staffordshire Bull Terrier
Welsh Terrier
West Highland White Terrier

Hound Group

Afghan Hound
Basenji
Basset Hound
Basset Fauve de Bretagne
Beagle
Bloodhound
Borzois
Dachshund (Long-Haired)
Dachshund (Miniature Long-Haired)
Dachshund (Miniature Smooth-Haired)
Dachshund (Wire-Haired)
Dachschund (Miniature Wire-Haired)
Deerhound
Elkhound
Finnish Spitz
Greyhound
Hamiltonstovare
Ibizan Hound
Irish Wolfhound
Otterhound
Petit Basset
Griffon Vendeen
Pharaoh Hound
Rhodesian Ridgeback
Saluki
Sloughi
Whippet

Working Group

Alaskan Malamute
Anatolian Shepherd Dog
Australian Cattle Dog
Bearded Collie
Belgian Shepherd Dogs (Groenendael, Laekenois,

Malinois and Tervueren)
Bernese Mountain Dog
Border Collie
Bouvier Des Flandres
Boxer
Briard
Bull Mastiff
Collie (Rough)
Collie (Smooth)
Doberman
Eskimo Dog
Estrela Mountain Dog
German Shepherd (Alsatian)
Giant Schnauzer
Great Dane
Hovawart
Hungarian Puli
Komondor
Lancashire Heeler
Maremma Sheepdog
Mastiff
Neopolitan Mastiff
Newfoundland
Norwegian Buhund
Old English Sheepdog
Pinscher
Polish Lowland Sheepdog
Portuguese Water Dog
Pyrenean Mountain Dog
Rottweiler
St. Bernard
Samoyed
Shetland Sheepdog
Siberian Husky
Swedish Vallhund
Tibertan Mastiff
Welsh Corgi (Cardigan)
Welsh Corgi (Pembroke)